PRAISE FOR
THIS SWEET EARTH

"*This Sweet Earth* is a much-needed book for this moment. This book comes alongside anyone with children in their lives who wants to face our current climate challenges with clear eyes and engaged hands, while also resting in the magic and wonder of this astoundingly beautiful earth."

—**Daneen Akers**, author of *Holy Troublemakers*
and Unconventional Saints and *Dear Mama God*

"When I first held my daughter all those years ago, pressing her tender pink skin against my tear-soaked face, I promised her that I would make a home for her. In retrospect, I lied: today, 'home' is no longer *at home*, and belonging is in crisis. The earth burns with the fires of its exhaustion, burdened by the weight of 'the human.'

With this precious pollination song, this wind-swept map-book, Lydia Wylie-Kellermann invites us to the fugitive vocation of wandering with our children—reminding us that it is in radical accompaniment that we might catch a glimpse of what they've always known, what my daughter seems to know now: that endings are strewn with stranger worlds, and the gift of our journeys lies not in arriving, but in the traveling together.

Read this book. And take your earthly leave for the awe tucked in the ordinary."

—**Báyò Akomolafe**, PhD, author of *These Wilds Beyond Our Fences:*
Letters to My Daughter on Humanity's Search for Home

"Reading *This Sweet Earth* made me hold my breath, then release it in a slow sigh of relief as my fears for the future were named openly. In this truthful and intimate meditation, Wylie-Kellerman leads us through grief and lament into a space of imagining how—whatever comes—we might choose to nurture communities of reciprocity where we, are and learn to thrive with less. This book left me feeling both calmer and braver, conscious that there is an alternative to the terrifying prospect of hunkering down behind walls and hoarding possessions. I am grateful for this different kind of hope."

—**Laura Alary**, author of *Here: The Dot We Call Home*
and *What Grew in Larry's Garden*

"Lydia Wylie-Kellermann surveys the flooded landscape of southwest Detroit, holding fast to her son's hand. The 'blunt edge of climate change' has come home. How do we raise resilient kids on a changing planet? Should we have children at all? Deeply insightful with exquisite, warm language. This gracious book echoes the political vision of the prophet Isaiah: 'And a little child shall lead them.'"

—**Rose Marie Berger**, author of *Bending the Arch:*
Poems and senior editor at *Sojourners* magazine

"Lydia Wylie-Kellermann invites us to pilgrimage and prayer walk, toddler walk and tween race, to stand in silent reverence and thunder like the holy prophets as we work to protect a world that is fragile, fractured, and still so fecund! Read this book aloud with friends and build community; share it with the kids in your life to start to see nature as they see her; read quietly to yourself, and your tears will cleanse, challenge, and change you. There is rich wisdom here, and wild reverence, and solemn joy. You will want to embroider these words onto fine linen, draw them in mandalas, ink them on your flesh, and magic-marker them onto big signs for the next protest!"

—**Frida Berrigan**, author of *It Runs in the Family: On Being Raised by Radicals and Growing into Rebellious Motherhood*

"This is no ordinary run-of-the-mill book on the environment. It is rather the wise, personal, up-close pondering by a woman of courage and honesty. Lydia Wylie-Kellerman says she writes as 'an ordinary mom.' Her kids are all over this book, asking, noticing, wondering. She takes time as a mom to consider both the majesty of creation and the reality of death. But she is at the same time a poet. The book teems with her poetry whereby she goes beneath our common clichés to new ways of truth-telling. She does not flinch from the hard stuff. She has been an activist all her life. It is her family legacy, and she lives it out with wisdom and patience.

This book is just right for community sharing, reflection, and worship—and eventually action. We may be grateful to this mom who has mobilized her life's work for this moment."

—**Walter Brueggemann**, author of many books including *The Prophetic Imagination* and William Marcellus McPheeters Professor of Old Testament at Columbia Theological Seminary

"Reading Lydia Wylie-Kellermann's writing often makes me weep. I feel a familiar longing for a world of tenderness, sacredness, and belonging that tugs at my heart and reminds me of my deep kinship with the world. While I joyfully welcome new nieces, nephews, and young friends into my life in these increasingly uncertain times, I am so grateful to have Lydia's questions, stories, and grounded example of how to walk forward with intention, curiosity, and hope."

—**Olly Costello**, artist

"When it comes to climate change, we're often reminded of the awful burden human life puts on our planet, and with that can come a real misanthropy. But *This Sweet Earth* offers stories and examples of how, even in moments of catastrophe, we can continue living together honestly and lovingly as part of creation. In a moment of catastrophe and a barrage of bad news, writing like Lydia's is an act of resistance, reminding us that, yes, another world is possible."

—**Dean Dettloff and Matt Bernico**, hosts of *The Magnificast*

"*This Sweet Earth* is a gentle love letter to future generations. Lydia Wylie-Kellerman takes a clear-eyed look at the current and coming impacts of global climate change and finds hope in the ordinary: neighborhood-scale mutuality, the fierce example of communities of color that have survived apocalypse already, and the sweet love and wonder of sweaty-headed boys for pet rabbits, bones found in the forest, and garden tomatoes."

—**Laurel Dykstra**, climate justice activist and author of
Wildlife Congregations: A Priest's Year of Gaggles,
Colonies and Murders by the Salish Sea

"*This Sweet Earth* is a banquet of hope and delight served on weighty platters of truth. With humor and poignancy, in poetry and prayer, through the voices of her children and her ancestors, Lydia Wylie-Kellermann graciously invites us all to the table. I highly recommend taking a seat and savoring her eloquent observations, her exquisite celebrations of simplicity and creativity, and her compelling honesty about parenting in an age of climate collapse."

—**Joyce Hollyday**, author of *Pillar of Fire*

"*This Sweet Earth* is exactly the book we need in this time of frightening changes in the world around us. Anchored in hope rather than despair, it heartens and inspires while remaining rooted in honesty and practicality. In elegant prose, Lydia Wylie-Kellerman turns her family's experiences into valuable lessons in nurturing community, exploring and preserving the natural world, and letting children lead as much as follow as we journey toward an uncertain future."

—**Michael N. McGregor**, author of *Pure Act: The Uncommon Life of Robert Lax*

"The deep tension between environmental despair and joy in the still-lovely-if-tattered creation we inhabit needs to be a source of energy for our efforts on its behalf. This account summons our best angels to the fore!"

—**Bill McKibben**, author of *The Comforting Whirlwind: God, Job, and the Scale of Creation*

"Weaving poetry, prose, and prayer, Lydia Wylie-Kellermann inspires us by recounting stories of her childhood and that of her two sons, refusing to turn away from the pain of our world. Lydia's upbringing in a community of faith and resistance provides the foundation for her children to grow up knowing that they are not separate from all of creation. Grounded in gratitude, she dares to tell the truth as she grieves with her sons the losses brought by the environmental crisis and helps them face even the possibility of near human extinction. In *This Sweet Earth*, Wylie-Kellermann invites us to open to our grief and outrage as we raise our children in the time of collapse, knowing that as we suffer with a suffering world, we find the strength and resilience to act on behalf of Earth."

—**Anne Symens-Bucher**, co-founder, Canticle Farm, Oakland, California

"Beautifully written and with poetry sprinkled throughout, *This Sweet Earth* weaves family stories, social analysis, and practical suggestions to all interested in preparing ourselves and our young people for this time of climate change. Much appreciation to author Lydia Wylie-Kellermann, who brings her humor, honesty, integrity, history, and earnestness, and calls all into hope, community, and the possibility for wholeness and repair in trying times."

—**Rev. Dr. Liz Theoharis**, co-chair of the Poor People's Campaign and editor of *We Cry Justice*

"Kids deserve the truth. Kids deserve the power to shape the way we live. Lydia Wylie-Kellermann helps us parents—who want more than anything to tell our kids, 'Everything is going to be okay,' when we know it won't—learn how to steer our kids toward light and life and the helpers, while resisting the systems built on greed. All while regulating our anxieties so they don't exacerbate our children's. Go get this important book."

—**Cindy Wang Brandt**, author of *Parenting Forward* and *You Are Revolutionary*

"Parenting through this climate crisis at times feels like a hopeless proposition. The grief, anger, and uncertainty can be overwhelming. What *This Sweet Earth* offers is permission to feel all of those emotions while giving a glimpse at what parenting can look like through the eyes of someone longing for a more just world. The moving reflections and prayers come through the much-needed voice of a poet, reminding us that the beauty of this world is worth fighting for."

—**Derrick Weston**, theological education and training coordinator for Creation Justice Ministries, and coauthor of *The Just Kitchen: Invitations to Sustainability, Cooking, Connection, and Celebration*

"Lydia Wylie-Kellerman loves children—hers, mine, and yours. How else could such a loving and wisdom-filled book be written with such compassion and skill? *This Sweet Earth: Walking with Our Children in the Age of Climate Collapse* is so desperately needed right now. Read it. Gift it to parents and grandparents and everyone who needs hope during this time of despair. This book is hope for our world and for the next seven generations!"

—**Randy Woodley**, author of *Becoming Rooted* and co-sustainer Eloheh Indigenous Center for Earth Justice

"How do we honor the lives and the words of our children? That is one graceful effort of *This Sweet Earth*. And in a strange likewise, it is the effort of this endorsement. Here is a beautiful book, a conversation between generations in a moment of earthly crisis. I am repeatedly astonished by the wise voices of my own grandchildren, never mind their mothers. I find myself herein (as I pray you might also). Even more, I see the parenting gifts of Lydia's mother, Jeanie Wylie, a writer whose clean and vivid prose have also been passed down. *This Sweet Earth* is an act of love. Collected like heirloom seed, scattered in reckless hope, rooted in warmed earth, and now harvested, fruit for the sharing. Taste and see."

—**Bill Wylie-Kellermann**, author of *Celebrant's Flame: Daniel Berrigan in Memory and Reflection* and *Principalities in Particular: A Practical Theology of the Powers That Be*

THIS SWEET EARTH

WALKING WITH OUR CHILDREN
IN THE AGE OF CLIMATE COLLAPSE

THIS
SWEET
EARTH

LYDIA WYLIE-KELLERMANN

Broadleaf Books
Minneapolis

Library of Congress Cataloging-in-Publication Data

Names: Wylie-Kellermann, Lydia, author.
Title: This sweet earth : walking with our children in the age of climate
  collapse / Lydia Wylie-Kellermann.
Description: Minneapolis, MN : Broadleaf Books, [2024] | Includes
  bibliographical references.
Identifiers: LCCN 2023058918 (print) | LCCN 2023058919 (ebook) | ISBN
  9781506495125 (print) | ISBN 9781506495132 (ebook)
Subjects: LCSH: Climatic changes--Psychological aspects. | Human
  beings--Effect of climate on. | Children and the environment. |
  Environmental psychology.
Classification: LCC BF353.5.C55 W95 2024 (print) | LCC BF353.5.C55
  (ebook) | DDC 155.9/15--dc23/eng/20240226
LC record available at https://lccn.loc.gov/2023058918
LC ebook record available at https://lccn.loc.gov/2023058919

Cover image: © 2023 Shutterstock; Forsythia branch. Golden Bell, blossoming
flowers. Hand drawn vintage vector illustration in black and white style. Can
be used for cards, invitations, banners, posters, print design./ 2149052487 by
InnaSakun. © 2023 Shutterstock; Abstract photocopy texture background with
dark edges/ 720382063 by Reddavebatcave © 2023 Shutterstock; silhouettes
of people, Collection, girls, Boys, children/631606187 by NadzeyaShanchuk
Cover design: Kimberly Glyder

Print ISBN: 978-1-5064-9512-5
eBook ISBN: 978-1-5064-9513-2

For Isaac and Cedar,
for Larkins Street,
and for this Sweet Earth to which we belong.

"For my grandchildren and other young folk, I'll one day, perhaps even soon, be an ancestor. *Pray for us, Bill*, they might one day chant and charge. I do so even now, already. I pray for the generations facing the cascading collapse of climate, the withering breakdown of things like truth, the social contract, and basic democracy. I pray for (or against) the things they will face. Indigenous peoples say famously that we should be living and praying seven generations down the line. Can those generations call on me to have their backs? Surround them with the cloud? Are we spiritually entangled? I light a candle for them, as they may light one for me. I will. I am. I'm there. (And thereby summoned to intercede with my body now.)"

—Grandpa Bill Wylie-Kellermann, "Ancestors Every Which Way: Praying With, As, and For the Saints."
Geez 70: Ancestors: Remembering Forward, Fall 2023

CONTENTS

CONTENTS

INTRODUCTION

All my life I have loved water. I can trace my spiritual journey by the waters I have known. But it isn't the big waters that call to me, but the tiny brooks tucked deep in the woods. The trickle of water moving over stones through the shadows of the forest. It has always been those little streams or small ponds that summon my body to come and rest awhile. If I am lucky enough to have pen and paper, it is there that I cannot help but pour out poetry attempting to capture the miraculous beauty of this world.

But lately, there is something different rising up in my body. I feel tension in my shoulders, creeping pain up the back of my neck. There is a pile of bricks on my chest, and my legs ache even when I have not walked a mile. I am gripped by anxiety as I listen to the news of yet another climate catastrophe, and despair lingers in my throat as I scan the next scientific report chronicling the ways in which things are worse than previously predicted. The ice caps are not regenerating ice. The ocean temperatures are too hot.

While you can see the evidence of climate change from one watershed to the next, you can also see the signs written along my spine and running through my veins. I am carrying this crisis in my body.

And on those days when I fear all is lost, it is not the trickle of streams summoning my body but the crashing waves of the Great Lakes. More than once, as a storm rolls in, I find myself in the car driving toward Lake Huron, desperately needing the wind and the waves.

I stand on the rocks and watch the storm dance with the water. The waves rise and crash. The wind tears through the trees along the shore. I let the waves splash against me and the wind whip my hair with abandon. The rain begins to pour so hard that I cannot distinguish between the raindrops and the tears that pour from my body.

Only in the vast power of water and sky can I find something powerful enough to ground my body. Here, as my small creaturely being stands along the shore, I release the tension and let the earth hold me.

We are living in an era of climate collapse. The weather and ecosystems all around us are changing. The catastrophes are becoming fiercer and more frequent. Most likely, it is too late to undo what has already been done.

So what now? How do we walk forward in this time? What does resistance look like? Is hope realistic? What does it look like for us to change everything about how we live?

And for those of us raising and loving kids, the questions only multiply. What does their future look like? What do they need to know? How can we hold their fear and anxiety when we struggle with our own?

And yet, somehow, it is these very children who are helping me live into these questions. And it turns out that holding their hands in this place and in this time has filled my heart with joy and left my body imbued with hope.

WOVEN IN THE EARTH

My children summoned this book out of me.

Their courage and their curiosity, their quietness and their wildness, and their laughter and their anger. The way their beings are so entwined with the world has changed me. They have altered my perspective, my imagination, my conscience, and my very vocation.

I watch my kids climb a tree or chase a seagull or rescue a spider or watch shooting stars, and I realize that my own body has grown disconnected from that knowing of being deeply woven into the depths of the earth.

In just a few short years with my kids, I have felt a sweeter intimacy and a sacred yearning to reweave my being back into this wild ecosystem to which I belong. I long to lie down in a field of clover to watch the honeybees. My heart yearns to sing in the wind. And when I hear the breeze in the willow tree, I know I am home. My kids' eyes and hearts and beings have forced me to give my life to the dandelion seed and the chrysalis and the chickadee calling my children's names.

GRATITUDE FOR THE OLD STREAMS

While there is no question that my kids' beings pulled this book from my bones, so much of the marrow I have found there came from the learnings absorbed in my own childhood.

I was raised by two incredible human beings—Bill and Jeanie Wylie-Kellermann. They were both writers, activists, and theologians. My sister and I grew up in southwest Detroit, just a few miles from where my dad was raised. He always talks about

Detroit as a vocation. The city was his teacher, and the struggles here are the work he is called to. His work shifted in his gut in 1967 when he stood on Grand River looking downtown as the city erupted in flames from the rebellion. At eighteen years old, his heart and imagination were claimed by this place.

My mom came to Detroit as a journalist with a bad habit of showing up on a picket line to report a story and getting arrested after joining the protest. She poured her heart into the Poletown community on the east side of Detroit as she documented the demolition of a Polish community by eminent domain to build yet another car factory. She joined the resistance as the community organized and fought to the bitter end to save their neighborhood.

These are the ones who raised me—two people who had Detroit woven into the fabric of their beings and were ready to give their bodies to the struggles for economic and racial justice.

And while my mom loved the city, her spirit also cried out for the wilderness. She had an unquenchable thirst for beauty and the earth. She loved the snow. We would put on snow boots and walk the winter trails until the sun went down. When the rain came, she would throw us in the car with our bathing suits and take us to the beach. We watched as others ran for their cars while we hauled inner tubes into Lake Huron delighting in the dark clouds and the pouring rain. She picked wildflowers and collected feathers. She had a spirituality that held reverence for the sanctuaries filled with candles; on the other hand, she created prayer circles of stones and cedar branches tucked in the forests.

When I was twelve, my mom collapsed with seizures, only to discover she had a stage 4 glioblastoma. Brain cancer. She was given less than a year to live. Miracle after miracle kept her alive for seven-and-a-half years. She died when I was nineteen. Those years that were filled with a roller coaster of surgeries and treatments formed me. Amid all the grief and hope, I woke up and found who I was. In those moments, I learned about the gift of being alive, of paying attention, of the sweetness of loving another human being so completely.

And now, almost eighteen years since she died, I find myself stumbling along similar paths and vocations. She was a journalist and an editor of *The Witness* magazine. I wouldn't have predicted this path, but I found my way to being editor of *Geez* magazine— a quarterly, ad-free, print magazine at the intersection of art, activism, and spirit. I love asking questions and gathering stories.

How I would love to have known my mom as an adult. She was fierce in the work of justice and gentle in the arms of the trees. She would have had incredible wisdom about what we are called to in this moment.

She would have loved my partner, Erinn. Erinn and I fell in love in the hillsides of France at Taizé monastery, where my mom spent time as a child. Erinn is a math nerd, a spoon carver, and a six on the Enneagram. After college, Erinn and I moved back onto the street where I grew up to build community and learn from the urban agriculture movement in Detroit.

I am so grateful for the ways I was raised. I am grateful for the endless stream of protests, from newspaper strikes to nuclear disarmament. I am grateful to have grown up worshiping in the Detroit Catholic Worker house, where mass took place in the living room of a hospitality house for homeless women and children. That is where I learned about what it means to break bread. I am grateful for the beloved families who all moved to that same block in southwest Detroit with commitments to simplicity and justice. Growing up with twenty other kids on the block and being loved by all those grown-ups changed everything for me.

All this to say that there is nothing new in this book. As my heart and body process climate change, so much of that bone marrow comes from what I learned as a child. The crisis may look different, the struggle may be on a different front, but the work and the lessons are the same.

I am grateful for the movements that have formed us all, going back generations. We owe everything to the hard-fought struggles for racial, economic, gender, sexuality, disability justice, and on and on. These struggles continue today, and they all intersect with this work of what it means to live humanly and equitably on this planet.

GO SLOW

My sister read some early pages of the book, and when I asked her what she thought, she said, "Tell your readers to go slow."

She was surprised by the emotions that were rising within her. She had to pick it up and then put it down. So yes, I urge you to read this book as slowly as you need. Listen to your heart and your body. Be gentle with yourself. That is so crucial in everything we do in this chaotic and uncertain time. Let this book be a place of company, rest, and love.

But also, moving slow is good advice for all of us for a million other reasons. Find that invitation tucked in the cracks of every page in this book.

So much of the culture that capitalism has created demands we speed up. Work faster. Shop faster. Scroll faster. Produce faster. Everything that is destroying the climate is moving too fast.

So perhaps, in order to choose another path for humanity, we need to start by simply slowing down. As writer and philosopher Bayo Akomalafe says, "When times are urgent, slow down."[1]

It turns out, as I look down the table of contents of this book, that slowness feels central to everything. Move slow to let ourselves grieve. Move slow to build community and meet our neighbors. Move slow to stumble upon the sacred. Move slow to discern what we create and how we resist. Move slow to honor the dead. Move slow and you cannot help but stumble upon gratitude. Move slow and release our creaturely beings to awe and wonder.

Slowness goes against everything we are taught and yet it may just save us . . . in more ways than one.

So dear friends,
indulge in slow time.
Lie down in the tall grasses
and feel the sun on your cheeks.
Listen for the cardinals who spend
their days singing to one another.
Marvel at the cicada climbing out of the dirt, into the tree,
and then slowly emerging from its old skin.
Wonder at the moon as she washes you with light
as you stand embraced by the darkness.
Stand amidst the circling snow of winter
and let the snowflakes on your tongue quench your thirst.
Pause amidst the children's endless questions
and wait to hear the answer they already know.
Trust that.
Go slow to find yourself

to be just another creature
in this wild and beautiful world.

LAND ACKNOWLEDGMENT OF DETROIT

The stories in this book take place in *Waawiyaatanong*, which means "where the river goes round." The land is now commonly known as Detroit, Michigan. The Wendat, an Iroquoian agricultural people living around Lake Erie, called this area *Teuchsa Grondie*, or "land of many beavers."[2]

When we talk about land justice and climate resilience, we cannot do so without acknowledging the role colonialism has played in the destruction, and without honoring the original land stewards who continue to care for this land. In this place, the Great Lakes Indigenous peoples include the Anishinaabe: Odawa, Ojibwe, and Potawatomi.

May we commit ourselves to actively making repair for the harm done to our Anishinaabe relatives, to being in right relationship with them, to walking well and carefully on this land, and to doing whatever we can to contribute to the thriving and sovereignty of both the Anishinaabe people and this beloved ecosystem.

A BLESSING FOR A CHILD

*A prayer poured from my heart after a late-night conversation
with my oldest,
who lay awake grieving what feels like the end of the world
and asked, "What would this land look like if the Europeans
had never settled here?"*

I know it feels scary sometimes.
I know it feels like everything is going wrong
and that the earth is in pain.
It's true.
It is so very true.
We can't pretend it away.
It is OK to be angry and to scream.
It is OK to be afraid and sad.
I feel that way too.
And I am here
to hold you
and love you.

But . . .
But . . .
what if . . .
we are actually
really lucky to be alive right now?
What if we learn,
like really learn,
from our mistakes
and our ancestors' mistakes?
What if we stand at a moment
where everything needs to change?
And what if we get to imagine ways of being
that are full of joy and imagination?
Ways of living that
keep the creatures safe
and make the earth sing?

I want to be there for that moment.
And I want to be there with you.
I want to witness
what you imagine,
what you dream,
what you inspire.
I want to witness
your courage
and your wonder
and your laughter.
And I don't ever
want you to feel alone
in any of it.

So beloved child,
let us take off our shoes
and walk upon this earth.
We can let the land hold us
just as we are.
There is no emotion too big,
no fear too terrifying
that the earth can't carry.

This earth holds so many stories
and remembers from so long ago.
I am glad I get to be
a small part of that story
with you.

1 | WADING INTO THE FLOOD

"The lights won't turn on!" We were shaken awake.

The cloudy morning had kept our room dark and drowsy, though I realized as I woke that I was damp with sweat. I stumbled out of bed following my kids over to the light switch. Sure enough—nothing. We moved around the house trying other switches, but it was clear the power was out. Last night, the rain fell hard and thunder roared.

We hurriedly got dressed and headed outside to see if others had also lost power. It was so uncannily quiet. Neighbors started drifting out of their houses.

"You have to see!" cried out a mom who lived a few houses down. She hurried us down to the end of the block that dead-ends at Interstate 94 in southwest Detroit.

The kids and I stepped up to the fence and looked down onto the six-lane freeway. My mouth dropped open. Nothing could have prepared me for what I saw.

Water. It was full of water. Signs and concrete dividers completely submerged. Construction barrels floated away, carried by the wind. All we could see was the top couple of feet of semi-trucks poking through the standing water.

My mind started racing. What *couldn't* I see? Were there cars disappeared below? Was everyone OK?

Stories began to be swapped along the fence. Neighbors had heard explosions around two in the morning and come out to see. The freeway had started filling with water fast, forcing people to abandon their cars and run up the hills onto our street. A truck driver had sat for hours in the pouring rain keeping an eye on his truck.

The water didn't move.

Over the course of the day, more news trickled in. The pump system was down. But even if it had been working there was nowhere for the water to go. The sewer system was overloaded. Seven inches of rain fell in an hour. The power was out throughout most of the city. Basements were flooded with several feet of rainwater and sewage. The cell phone grid was down.

Our family, along with our neighbors, stood there for hours in shock as we watched rescue divers swim through the freeway searching buried cars for bodies.

It was the blunt edge of climate change staring us in the face.

THEY WILL NEVER KNOW

When I was young, my dad used to go out on a cold winter's night with a hose to drench our little yard in Detroit. He would do it again in the morning and then again that night. After a few days, my little sister and I would have our very own skating rink. We would spend hours and weeks circling the swing set and ducking under the apple tree. Twenty-five years later, my kids know that apple tree well, having climbed to the top dozens of times. But they will never know what it is to skate beneath her branches. The climate has shifted. Winters oscillate between unseasonable warmth and sudden deep freezes. It doesn't stay cold long enough for a skating rink.

On a little lake in northern Michigan, my friend and I would wade into the water, keeping our eyes out for creatures. We would set traps for crayfish, grab clams with our hands, and scoop up leeches in cups. Minnows. Toads. Frogs. Tadpoles. For a few days, we would host a living museum that we charged our parents a nickel to see. Then we would release them back into the lake. I bring my own kids to this lake each year, but there are no clams, no leeches, no tadpoles. They still hunt for minnows and attempt to catch fish, but the biodiversity of the lake has languished.

CARRYING GRIEF AND ANXIETY

Climate change is all around us. We feel it in little ways, like how we harvest the cherries in our yard a little earlier each year. And in the big ways, as we worry for friends out west as fires blaze, sweeping through whole towns. In Detroit, we have had not one but a dozen hundred-year storms in the last five years. I witness my friends, who are environmental justice warriors in this city, fall down in exhaustion and something too close to despair. The war to privatize water rages on in Detroit as we are nestled in 20 percent of the world's fresh water while other places have begun to run dry.

The rains fall harder. The snow comes less frequently. Aqueducts are drying up. Fires burn. The air grows toxic. The songbirds are growing quiet. The red knots cannot find food. The black-footed ferrets are vanishing. The monarchs' migratory path is endangered. The persistent trillium blooms less and less.

3

The mountaintops are being harvested. Topsoil is drifting away. Plastic fills the oceans.

I scroll through climate reports and scientific studies predicting the date for human extinction. There are moments I don't feel like I can breathe.

It's too much. This loss lives in our bodies. There is reason to weep. And a collective need to hold it.

Anxiety and grief are real. They're immobilizing. And in my experience, those feelings are only growing daily as it seems like one weather disaster after another strikes. I could not have imagined days on end not being able to let my kids play outside because the air quality was so bad from forest fires hundreds of miles away.

How do I hold my own feelings of grief and anxiety while also trying to be a parent? I fear for their future. How on earth are we supposed to nurture children in this moment? So many of us have already tasted climate catastrophe; if we haven't, we will soon. Sometimes it feels like we are moving from one crisis to the next without time to catch our breath.

And then I reach for the hand of my six-year-old who leads me over to watch a cicada emerging from its own skin. Following his lead, I still my body and welcome the quiet. His awe and wonder are infectious, and I feel my spirit shift. My nine-year-old kneels down beside us, his feet covered in dirt. He has refused to wear shoes outside for the past two months because he argues he "can better communicate with the earth." My kids are shifting my posture. They have brought my body closer to the earth and reminded me of the place to which I belong. I am grateful for these sacred child teachers whose lives are intimately wrapped up in mine. I am taking notes daily as they name that which I had not seen.

HAUNTING QUESTIONS

For those of us whose lives are intimately wrapped up with children, how do we stay grounded? What do we tell them? What skills will they need?

These questions haunt my dreams and linger as I do the dishes. They are the questions that each of us experiment with throughout our lives. Like flotsam and jetsam on the seaside, I am gathering stories, questions, and experiments. I write them down in this place to add to a holy conversation of which each of us is a part. We need one another. We need one another's company. We rely on one another's dreams. And we work to remember that we are not alone.

I do not believe that the education with which I was raised—education that came in the form of desks and bells and memorization—will offer them much as they walk into this unknown future. They need to know the names of the songbirds and to have looked them in the eye. They need to know how to care for animals and put seeds in the ground. They need to be able to find joy in the midst of chaos. They need to know how to tend to the dying and honor the dead.

WRITING FROM A POSITION OF SYSTEMIC POWER

I am a white woman with myriad privileges writing about climate catastrophe that disproportionately affects the lives of Black and brown folks, folks living with disabilities, and those surviving on the edge of the economic crisis. My own ancestral lines and the culture of whiteness itself bears the bulk of responsibility for where we find ourselves in the climate crisis.

Many of the branches of my ancestral tree moved from England, Scotland, and Ireland into the hills of Pennsylvania as early as the mid-1600s. I am slowly learning and remembering this history. But I know that within my blood and bones I carry the memory of the Lenni Lenape people being violently forced off these lands. It was those days that shifted how these forests and hills were cared for and understood. Instead of humans belonging to the land, the land belonged to humans. That shift in consciousness as white men seized brutal control of what is now called the United States led to forests fallen, swamps drained, streets paved, factories built, and water poisoned. We can trace the white supremacy right into factory farms, capitalism, plastics, nuclear weapons and waste, and on and on.

The lost connection to the land spun climate change out of control. My ancestors, my blood, my body hold that memory. To do this work, we must remember, reconcile, reconnect, reimagine, and reground ourselves with the land and creatures of this place.

As a white person living on this land carrying the ancestral lines that I do, it is perhaps all the more important that I look this crisis in the eye, in its history, and join a different path.

LOVING CONFESSIONS

As I write, I want to be clear: I am no expert. I am merely a parent who feels grief and who tries to keep my eyes open. I am a daughter who has learned bone lessons about justice and place from my own parents. I am a partner who is constantly in communication about the monotonous and miraculous of the everyday and the state of the world. I am a writer who processes my heart by putting words down on a page and who searches for the sacred. I am a question-asker and story-gatherer. I hope to name aloud the hungers so many of us hold.

This book is also sprinkled with stories about my kids. Isaac is nine, and from the day he was born it seemed like he was more at home in nature. As an infant, when he would start to scream or cry, he would calm down if we walked outside. Cedar is six and alive in his body. He can climb the tallest tree and cartwheel through the fields.

And while there are moments of magic that wind through these pages, you should also know they are your regular kind of kids. They drive me crazy. They *still* wipe their boogers on my shirt. They break stuff and kick soccer balls at the car. There is an endless stream of fart jokes, big feelings that often lead to kicking and screaming, and excruciating stubbornness. But we love them.

I am endlessly grateful that I get to parent with my partner Erinn, whose own vocations have varied from finding the equation needed to calculate the velocity of a river and understanding the mechanics of combined sewer systems to picking up fallen logs and a knife to carve beautiful spoons. She can be brought to tears by the wind blowing through wild grasses. We love to dream together, to ask the hard questions, and to face parenting as a grand and difficult adventure.

And you must be under no illusion. I am a regular old mom. I've let them have too much screen time and too much sugar. I struggle with saying no and holding boundaries. But through and within all the ordinariness, we are trying to pay attention . . . to the news and our neighborhood, to our spirits and our stories, to the cherry blossoms and our collective dreams.

This is a book about wandering with children in the climate collapse. It names our fears and our rage, our grief and our hope. It is about sacred attention and earthly intimacy. It is about how we struggle and what we create. It is about community and falling in love with the place where we stand. It dares to believe that there is space for gratitude and overwhelming joy. Through it all, these pages sing out for us to be alive on this sweet earth.

So dear friends,
welcome.
Move slow through these pages.
Take up these stories
and put them down.
Tend to your own stories.
Notice the seasons changing.
Let your eyes linger on the children in your life.
Squander your attention
on their fingers and toes
and the places they go.
In these dangerous times,
watch for magic.

A BLESSING FOR YOU NOW

Tucked in you is the beauty
of all that ordinary and extraordinary.

Embrace this wandering journey.
May we relish the questions,
honor the old stories,
create new stories,
cry, laugh, delight
and walk gently
into all that is
to come.

2 | CHOOSING LIFE IN THE FACE OF DEATH

"Why do you want to be parents?"

I smirked while trying to keep chewing a mouthful of roasted vegetables. I put my fork down.

Erinn and I were hosting two beloved friends, Luke and Joan, for a celebratory dinner. This week, we would start trying to get pregnant. The four of us had been meeting for months about Luke being our sperm donor. We knew that since they were together, it was truly a gift from both of them. We were navigating dreams, permissions, logistics, and commitments to one another. It was three years before gay marriage would be legalized, so we wandered through messy conversations about legalities. We were forced and gifted with needing to lean into the trust of friendship and community. The friendship was deep and long and we trusted one another to the unknowns that would surely emerge in the years to come.

Erinn and I were never going to get pregnant by accident. If we were going to have kids, it would be a very intentional act.

So I should have been prepared for the question.

"Why do you want to be parents?" Joan asked.

A pregnant pause hung in the air as the beets, carrots, and garlic from our backyard garden delighted my tongue.

Why did I want to have kids? Terrifying flashes flew before my eyes—families fleeing in their cars ahead of fires wiping their way through towns. Children hiding under their desks during yet another school shooting. The faces of Black children killed by police miles from our house. The pollution pouring out of the Marathon plant down the road. Another mass shooting at an LGBTQ nightclub. Children an hour north suffering lead poisoning from their drinking water and children in my own neighborhood living without running water because their families couldn't afford it. Did I really want to bring kids into this world?

How can we bring children into a world that is on fire? How can we choose·to have a kid when fresh water is becoming scarce and air quality is plummeting? Will it be too hot for them to ride their bikes outside in the summer? Are there even enough resources on the planet for a child in this ever-growing population? Is it even ethical to have children?

So many people I know are carrying these questions. The very questions hold crippling anxiety, unbearable anger, and unbelievable grief. There is a hardness in the truth of knowing that although it is not the choices of our generation that led us to this moment, we are the ones who will feel the loss. I know lots of folks who have decided they cannot have kids because of climate change, despite a lifetime of longing for them. That grief is palpable.

There are no right answers here. No tidy lists of shoulds or should nots. We all have to find ways to honor the questions. To listen for the voices lingering in our longings. To discern and imagine the impacts of our choices. There are a million pieces to consider, some of which are universal and some of which are intimately personal. We choose what feels right in our bones.

And we trust one another to those choices. We must release judgment of ourselves and those around us. No matter which way we move, there is deep, undeniable grief.

But for us, when Joan asked the question, "Why do you want to be parents?" it poured out. Joy and words flowed from our lips.

"I feel the yearning in my body crying out for children."

"Love is abundant and we want to wrap it around a baby."

"We want to see how it changes us, how it changes our relationship, to see who we become."

"We want to widen our community, bringing children in as our teachers, partners, and companions for whatever lies ahead."

"We want to lean into joy and wonder and awe."

On and on our words carried us. It was a full body, full heart, full spirit choice that rippled around the table that night and into the days to come.

There were no doubts for us. There was fear. Fear around our abilities. Fear around homophobia and what it would feel like for our kids to have two moms. Fear around what their futures would look like in a time of climate change. But there were no doubts.

The whole process turned out to be a deepening of community. A beautiful expanding of the definitions and possibilities of family. It was easy to lean on one another. And the love between all of us only grew.

EMBRACE THE MESS

As I look back now, that process was not bad learning for the climate crises we might face in the future. Systems and laws will likely not be there to save us. Institutions will crumble. Instead, we will be forced to lean into relationships and community for our survival. Life will be messy and filled with uncertainty. What a gift it is when we can practice those skills now. Lean into the mess. Trust our neighbors. Solve problems around undeniably complicated matters of life.

And gosh darn it, amid the constant realities of injustice and collapse, I'm so glad we said yes to being parents!

I can no longer imagine the fabric of the ecosystem of which I am a part without these living, growing beings. I am so grateful for the ways their existence has intensified my actions, grounded my hope, and welcomed my grief. I have fallen madly, completely in love with them. They have made it impossible not to fight like hell for a future for them and the generations to come after. Isaac and Cedar have given me reason to delight in each moment. They have awakened within me the power to love abundantly and fiercely.

These lovely, infuriating, human boys of ours' have already been such gifts to community and this planet. And I hope, as we pour love into their bodies, that they never doubt their belonging, their goodness, their gift of life on this sweet earth.

THROUGH THE PASSAGE

A few years ago, I was editing an issue for *Geez* magazine on climate justice. It was one of those watershed moments for me, when my anxiety and grief were at their height. I was walking around with a toddler on my hip and a chatty kindergartener, but all I could feel were the constant bricks on my chest. My doomsday scrolling had left me numb.

I was working on an interview for the issue with Joanna Macy over the phone. Joanna Macy is an environmental activist and a scholar of Buddhism, systems theory, and deep ecology.

I wasn't asking the questions but was tucked in the next room with headphones recording the conversation. And it was a good thing I didn't have to do the talking, because as her ninety-year-old voice traveled through the airways, I began to cry. "Of course you're scared!" she said. "Look those fears straight in the eye. Don't try to avoid them. Because something momentous is happening, not only for our climate, but to the whole industrial growth society of corporate capitalism. . . . But I believe this just had to come. Because it's devouring our earth . . . and my own feeling is, the sooner the better. Every extracted mine, every new smokestack, every new factory—even if they're renewables—all of them are mining earth, exhausting earth, and dimming our hopes."[1]

Macy had this incredible gift of being so clear about the devastation and immediate danger we were in, while also radiating hope and joy.

"It's going to take a big toll because our natural survival skills have been weakened. But they're not gone, and we are plugged into a powerful and resourceful living planet. . . . There is a lot we have to relinquish, but it's fantastic! So take a deep breath and don't close down."

I heard the plea in her voice. I knew she was right. It is so easy to close down. I feel that desire in myself and I see it in those I love. The bricks on my chest want to force me under the covers. Or other days, I want to look away and pretend I can go on living as if this isn't happening.

"I personally feel incredibly grateful to be alive in this moment, and to have lived this long, that I can take part in this immense possibility of transformation of our life on earth from a killing society to a radiant renewing society."

I felt her words trickle through my whole body. That is the gratitude I want to live with. That is the imagination I want to cultivate. Are we, in fact, lucky to be alive right now? Do we stand at a moment that needs community and creativity and radical change? Can our lives be part of the magic that has to happen? Perhaps we face a wild and wonderful adventure as we continue to choose all sorts of forms of life in the midst of death?

I felt breath move through my chest, releasing just a bit of the weight that lived there. Yes, that is the moment where we stand. We don't have another choice. No other choice but to lean into loving our neighbors and the watersheds that nurture us and welcome whatever is to come.

Then we broached with Macy this predicament that so many young folks are carrying about whether to have kids in this moment.

She paused for a minute and then spoke, "I'm grateful for those who choose mindfully, with clear understanding, to bear children into this time. Because we're going to need those newcomers coming in through the passage of collapsing society, carrying the grief, and moving forward into a life-sustaining culture that can be born of this."

More tears fell from my eyes. I've carried those words with me for the last three years, and each day I find them to be more true. My kids, as young as they are, don't carry the same baggage that I do. The cultural addictions to capitalism, individualism, and white supremacy don't look the same for their lives. Isaac and Cedar both feel the earth's pain and want to act. They feel their bodies as part of the ecosystem. They easily remember the names of plants and toads and mushrooms. They already know so much I did not.

I give thanks every day for them. I am grateful to have taken the risks, to have walked toward our fears, and to have expanded our community.

NOTHING NEW

As I write, I am reminded of words from writer and cultural organizer in Detroit Owólabi Aboyade. When *Geez* printed a piece about raising kids in a troubled world that asked these very questions, he pushed back hard.

Owólabi wrote, "For many who grew up in conditions of genocide, raising the next generation can be a sort of duty. The arguments against 'overpopulation' and the (white) doubts of 'raising kids in a troubled world' never meant much to me. My folks made it through invasion, capture, enslavement, fascism and did their damnedest to prepare the next generation to continue the family energy, and I am proud to do the same."[2]

He is not the first to call bullshit on our white naivete. It is not a new thing to worry about your children's survival, but perhaps it is newer to many of us white folks. This is not the first crisis. This is not the first generation to face death. Through generations, folks have found it within them to choose life.

CHOOSING TO BE HERE NOW

And there are infinite ways of choosing life in the face of death. It doesn't have to be kids. We all find the life that calls to our bones.

Perhaps we nourish life by putting pen to paper or hands in the dirt. Perhaps we help those who are dying to walk with joy, or a classroom of kids to sing a little louder, or by feeding the birds. Perhaps we have claimed the title of aunt, uncle, godparent, neighbor, or friend to a beloved child. All of it is necessary.

Having kids has been one way for me to pour out my love in celebration of life. It has not made the grief lighter . . . perhaps it has deepened it. But it has also expanded my hope, my joy, my longings, and my insistence on what is possible in this moment. Community and imagination are powerful forces and gosh do these kids know how to call upon it. Don't look away from death, but in its midst, choose life. Choose life. Choose life.

I end with these words from friend, mentor, healing practitioner Marcia Lee, who wrote these words during pregnancy, shortly after she and her partner, en, had a miscarriage. Life and death, grief and joy were tangibly connected.

"Life has been, and will always be, defined by death. And in these days when capitalism and white supremacy push an inhospitable, hostile system, destruction and suffering seem even more present. At times I am fraught with fear and guilt about bringing another human into this world. But more and more, I am leaning into faith that this child's soul is choosing to be here now, that they can contribute more in these times by coming into the physical realm than not, and that I can trust in our (be)loved community to (imperfectly) commit to live in the world our children need. As my body changes and this soul grows inside of me, I am also recognizing that the more I embrace that death will come, the more freely I can live daily in joy, love, generosity, and commitment to community and justice. As en reminds me, 'The moment life begins it also begins to die. And ultimately, life wants to live.'"[3]

> Dear friends,
> ask the hard questions.
> Give thanks for uncertainty.
> Trust yourself.
> Lean into the wisdom of community.
> Don't take yourself too seriously.
> Know that the arc is long.
> Lean on the ancestors.
> Ask the creatures for advice.
> Follow the wind.
> Know that there is no right way.
> Trust others on their path.
> Find yours.
> Embrace the mess.
> Give your life to a
> holy, undeniable "Yes!"
> Whatever that yes may be.
> And know, that this "had to happen."
> How lucky we are to be alive!

A BLESSING FOR THE RIVER OF LIFE

> Wrapped in the grief,
> tucked inside the questions,
> hidden in the unknown,

dwells fertile soil.
Give yourself
to that life
which you cannot yet know.
You are not the first.
You will not be the last.
Step into this flowing river.
Step in.

3 | CAN'T SAVE WHAT YOU DON'T LOVE

"Sandhill cranes!" Isaac shouted from the back seat.

I slowed the car down and turned into the parking lot of a county park where two sandhill cranes and their two babies were wandering between the cars. They truly are mysterious and glorious birds that seem to resemble creatures from the age of dinosaurs.

I parked and we all hopped out to marvel at this family. Slowly the cranes moved off the parking lot and began to walk down a trail. The four of us followed at a distance. Eventually the sandhill cranes got engrossed in some seeds on the ground that had fallen from a tree.

We tiptoed around them and continued along this unknown trail. We strolled for ten minutes or so finding fox poop, a painted turtle, and deer tracks.

And then we stopped in our tracks as we looked ahead on the trail to see a mom and her son. He must have been about ten and sat in his wheelchair with his hand outstretched while a bird sat right on his hand. The four of us looked at one another in amazement. How did he get that bird to land in his hand? We didn't move for fear the bird would fly away.

A few minutes later, the mom and son continued on the trail. As they passed us the mom said, "Would you like some bird seed?" And she handed us a Ziplock bag. "Thank you!"

We stepped up to where the boy had been and poured bird seed into our own hands. And then we waited. And waited. And waited some more.

Then suddenly, a chickadee landed right on Cedar's hand. He was only four at the time, but he stood perfectly still, with a grin wrapped around his face, gently whispering, "hello chickadee."

It wasn't long before Isaac had a tufted titmouse coming for a seed, flying away, coming back for another. I couldn't believe it when a downy woodpecker landed right on my finger. The bird was so light and her talons so gentle.

It was magic. These tiny creatures hide in the trees offering a soundtrack to our days that we so often miss. Yet here they were resting in the palm of our hands, honoring us with their fragile, miraculous beings.

Little did we know that this was a trail where many visited to feed the birds. The birds knew this as a trusted place to eat out of travelers' hands. I do not doubt that this is complicated and perhaps not the safest for the birds. But those brief moments we had with those birds changed us. I love watching my kids fall madly in love with this world. They walk with such tenderness and joy spewing out animal facts I can never remember. As I watch my kids, I think they hold a different relationship to creation than I did as a child. They do not seem to put a divide between nature and humans. My kids see themselves as part of nature, in real relationship with the creatures and the trees.

We lingered on that trail for hours. Erinn and I grew antsy and ready to go, but Isaac and Cedar didn't want to be any other place on earth. They had both lain down on the ground with their hands full of seeds. It wasn't long before the juncos and chipmunks were eating out of their hands.

LEARN THIS PLACE

When I think about parenting in this moment, I often think about the words from the Senegalese environmentalist Baba Dioum, who said, and I paraphrase, "You can't save a place you don't love. You can't love a place you don't know. And you can't know a place you haven't learned."[1]

I think that is some of the most important and radical work we can do as parents of young kids: help them learn the land that holds them. By doing so we are nurturing them to fall in love with this place—and ultimately that love may lead to imagination and action for climate justice.

In moments when I am overwhelmed or worried about what I should be teaching our kids, I find these words incredibly hopeful. Help our kids learn this place. We can do that.

So we lie down on our bellies and watch the milkweed disappear as the caterpillar grows fat. We wander the neighborhood in search of snacks in the form of wild grape vines, tiger lilies, and the roots of Queen Ann's lace. We throw lavish funerals for the fallen sparrow and delight when the opossum comes to visit. We have had far too many temporary visitors to count, keeping them in carefully designed climates—toads, worms, spiders, injured birds, and an occasional salamander. We let mud get between our toes and we climb the apple trees. With each moment, we are learning this place. We are all falling in love.

CALLING THE CHICKADEE BY NAME

Cedar and I love to fill the bird feeders, especially in the winter. Our bird identification book has grown tattered as we have now learned by heart the names including house finch, Baltimore oriole, cardinal, and red-bellied woodpecker. These were some of the kids' earliest words and they cried them out in their full syllable glory whenever one of these creatures appeared on our porch.

Three billion birds have gone missing in the US and Canada since 1970. Ninety percent of those are species we see on a daily basis—sparrows, blackbirds, warblers, finches. Ninety-two million red-winged blackbirds alone have disappeared.[2]

I think about those breathtaking creatures sitting on my hand that day. We humans continue to ruin the ecosystems, creating a place where birds can no longer survive. Species are shrinking and disappearing everywhere. The bug diversity has diminished so much since I was a child. And I worry that so much of this is happening without us even noticing.

And it's not only creatures, birds, and trees being wiped out, but language itself. We are forgetting their names. The *Oxford Junior Dictionary* regularly evaluates which words to include in the limited pages of their book based on what children most need to know. Over the past fifteen years, there has been an influx of technology words: "broadband," "email," and "cut and paste." And what words came out to make room? "Acorn," "willow," and "dandelion." In 2007, the *Oxford Junior Dictionary* removed more than fifty nature words, and it removed another fifty in 2012.

Robert Macfarlane wrote and Jackie Morris illustrated a gorgeous book called *The Lost Words*, which grieves the shifts in our language. They tenderly focused on each eliminated word with poetry and art: "bluebell," "fern," "kingfisher," and "otter."

These words are not "necessary" or commonplace for children anymore. They are not being taught. They are not being learned. What does this say about our culture when the natural world is not understood as crucial to our surroundings or to our survival? And what is the cost?

How will our children notice the blue herons disappearing if they don't even know what they are called?

Naming becomes a way of remembering, of paying attention, of determining what has value in our lives. The simple act of language becomes resistance. So we learn their names. We look. We listen. We sit still. We call them by their names. White-throated sparrow. Northern cardinal. Mourning dove. So that if they start to go silent, we will notice.

LOVE THIS PLACE

A couple of years ago, Cedar and I made birdseed wreaths as Christmas gifts. We mixed birdseed and peanut butter and gelatin together and poured it in a Bundt pan, decorating the edges with cranberries and cedar branches. And then, with the leftover seed, we rolled little balls together and let them dry on the counter.

On Christmas morning, once our presents were unwrapped and our bellies full, we pulled on snow pants and boots and hopped in the car to head to one of our favorite trails that winds its way around a small lake. In the spring, we would visit the turtles and bull frogs. But now the lake was beginning to freeze over and we knew the frogs and fish were deep below the icy surface, breathing ever so slowly, awaiting the thaw that would come in a few moons.

Along the trail, we still spotted creatures who love the winter in this place. Those creatures that don't migrate to warmer places or tuck under the soil. There were deer paths in the snow and squirrels scurrying up tree trunks, and, oh, how those cardinals' red feathers reverberated through my being as they sat on snow covered branches.

The kids reached into my pocket, each grabbing a bag filled with the bird seed balls Cedar and I had created a few days earlier. They ran ahead searching for spots to leave them. They found crooks in trees and little holes in fallen logs. They left some on rocks beside the water.

"We are leaving Christmas gifts for the birds and the squirrels!" Cedar shouted.

Fall in love.

Fall madly, deeply, uncontrollably in love with the place where your body lands. Love the land and creatures that surround you so much that your heart could burst.

Perhaps one of the cultural elements that has increased our disconnection to land in our society is how transient we have become. It is not uncommon to move across the country or across the city for a job, a house, or a better school district. It has meant that we so often don't know our neighbors. And we certainly don't know the ecosystem. It makes it harder to love a place and also to notice changes over time.

For our family, we wanted roots. We wanted to know and learn and love a place. We wanted to know the feeling of belonging to a place and letting that place belong to us. We wanted our lives to be about reciprocity.

So we landed on this block in southwest Detroit. The same one where I was raised. Just a few miles from where my dad grew up. My kids have climbed the same trees, skinned their knees on the same broken sidewalks, and put the same fistfuls of lead-infested dirt into their mouths as toddlers when we weren't looking. I have watched their bodies grow over the years alongside the apricot tree. And when we leave Christmas presents tucked in the crooks of the trees for the birds, they are for creatures the kids know, in places they return to again and again.

Place matters. Roots matter.

Daniel Berrigan, a Jesuit peace activist now a beloved ancestor, once said "Don't just do something. Stand there." Standing in one place and not moving is a part of the work. And a beautiful piece that leads to knowledge and intimacy and relationship. Resistance to climate destruction can be slow work of being present to a place in the face of a transient, fast-paced world.

Fall in love.

None of us are going to save this planet alone. But we can shift patterns of destruction in our own ecosystem. If we learn the place and fall madly in love, how could we not interfere in the destruction and make change?

NOTICED IN THE CRACKS

In the summer of 2021, my dad, the boys, and I biked down to the Detroit River. Beside the flowing water, elders led us in communal mourning. Over the previous few months, we had gained a great many ancestors in our community who had crossed over due to pandemics of Covid-19 and racialized police violence. Detroit had been hit hard. The disproportionate effect on people of color was evident in the lengthy list of names cried out on the riverbanks that day.

While my dad and I stood listening, Isaac and Cedar ran and climbed into imagined worlds on the edges of the gathering. There is something beautiful about allowing them to be kids, while also having them show up. I trust that even on the outskirts they are being formed by the words and rituals.

Soon, there was a tugging on my arm. "Come, come." I didn't want to step away from the powerful eulogizing, but their pull was insistent.

They dragged me over to the fountain that had been dry for many years. "Here, here." They led me to the corner of the drain where, tucked in the cracks, was a wing and a leg and a beak. "It's a baby robin," they said. Hundreds of people must have passed by, but I doubt anyone else had noticed the bird.

Death. It fills all our cracks in seen and unseen places. And while I had wanted to tend to my own grief, their persistent summoning led me to another memorial that honored another place where tears and presence were needed.

I rose from the ground offering my kids gratitude for the noticing and for the invitation. I walked away to rejoin the circle of grown-up mourners. As I walked away, Cedar cried out "Tell Grandpa to come. We need him to pray over the bird."

These children have fallen in love with this place. They know the creatures. They call them by name. And they are noticing when a tiny, beloved bird goes missing.

Dear friends,
Love the chickadee, the heron,
the eagle, and the sparrow.
Pledge your allegiance
to the woodruff, the fern,
the poisonous ivy,
and the bleeding hearts.
Say their names.
Don't forget.
Keep watch.
Touch them.
Taste them.
Smell them.
Fall in love.

With a small hand in yours
walk into the wild.
Guide their hand to the bark of a tree.
Witness a whole world
living in these woody layers.

A BLESSING FOR TRANSFORMATION

May you ride
on the wings of curiosity.
May wonderment
lead to listening,
lead to learning,
lead to loving.
And let that change
everything.

4 | COMMUNITY CHANGES EVERYTHING

We didn't know how our lives would change when we got baby chicks.

This was years before our kids were born. Before we were married. With dreams of intentional community, Erinn and I had moved to the block I grew up on in Detroit. With other recent college grads, we made commitments around common meals, life-sharing, hospitality, and work in the neighborhood. It was messy. We made mistakes. Sometimes we moved too fast and had to learn the beauty of slowing down. But we also loved one another and the neighborhood.

In those early days, we brainstormed how we could get to know more of our neighbors. Should we deliver bread? Make a flyer? Sit on the porch? Despite all our planning, it turned out to be chickens that would seal the deal on community.

These tiny, fuzzy creatures lived in a cardboard box smelling up our basement. But each day, we would bring them out into the backyard for some spring sunshine. On that first day, a brother and sister who were five and eight years old wandered back, having heard a rumor that there were chicks. We placed a baby chick in their hands and they squealed with delight, "it tickles!"

The next day they came with two more kids. Suddenly, our yard was full of kids playing tag and carrying chicks around like babies. All the chicks were being named. When the sun started to set, parents wandered back in search of their kids. As twilight fell, we began to learn one another's names and share our stories.

That was the beginning for us. Those conversations turned into potlucks in our backyard, and then homework help for kids after school, and then grocery runs for elders.

The following year, the neighborhood held its first block party. We worried we weren't organized enough, but it turned out that you just had to set a date and let folks know. On the day of the party, neighbors poured out of their houses with tables and chairs and food to share. We had sidewalk chalk and face paint. There was a donut-eating contest and musical chairs (the adult game was always a little too competitive for me). The grill would burn for hours and hours, wafting delicious smells through the neighborhood. And then, once the kids went to bed, a neighbor always brought his karaoke machine onto the porch and people would sing and dance long into the night.

The next morning, as we picked up chairs and pulled in garbage cans, I was always amazed at the simplicity and beauty of community. It took my breath away. Our neighbors were all so different, from such different walks of life . . . different politics . . . different religious backgrounds . . . different socioeconomic realities. And yet, joy poured out. We knew we could lean on one another.

The years rolled by. We continued to hold block parties and light parades and neighborhood garage sales. We organized trick-or-treating and put up a neighborhood altar for Día de los Muertos.

And we loved one another through the hard and beautiful times. Neighbors came to our wedding despite their church's teachings on sexuality. And we showed up when friends were picked up by ICE (Immigration and Customs Enforcement), posting bond, offering rides, and helping with kids when a parent was deported. We held candlelit gatherings when violence occurred in our neighborhood.

Our lives have become inextricably bound up with one another's.

LOCAL ECONOMIES

One day in mid-June, a neighbor wandered over while we were playing in the yard. He asked if he could pick cherries from our tree. "Of course!" He brought over a ladder and picked a bag full of cherries. When he left, he handed us a five-dollar bill.

Later that night, his eleven-year-old son knocked on our door asking if we wanted to buy a pupusa dinner. "Of course!" He handed over a container with two pupusas and sides of refried beans and rice. And I handed him that same five-dollar bill.

In that moment, I recalibrated my own understanding of economics. This was local economy. Figuring out how to keep as many dollars as possible circulating among our neighbors.

That summer, on our sidewalk—which sat in the middle of our two-block neighborhood—we started a farmers market. The kids helped me drag out chairs and tables each Wednesday afternoon. We would bring whatever overabundance was growing in our yard: grapes, pears, lavender, and eggs from our chickens.

One neighbor brought kale, beets, and tomatoes. Another neighbor brought a cooler full of fresh queso and tamales. Sometimes there were medicinal tinctures and handmade soap. And there was always honey, so much honey! Folks would pull up a chair and talk for two hours, and then we would all trade some dollar bills and go home with arms full of the gifts of earth and community.

The local economy just kept growing. We paid teenagers to do yard work and contracted with neighbors for plumbing and construction jobs. One household runs a bakery out of their house each Sunday and another has a restaurant in their basement on weekends.

We can give less of our money to the corporations and keep money in our local communities . . . even the tiniest of local communities, right in our neighborhood. With each small act, we deepen relationships and lighten the load on the earth.

There are also ways we can pull money right out of the equation. We share lawn mowers, shovels, and washing machines. We have painting parties and help one another stack wood. By relying on community, we can live with less money, less stuff, and create less waste.

When we first moved to the neighborhood, we didn't have a TV, so every Thursday our neighbor would invite us over to watch *Grey's Anatomy*. About twelve of us would gather to watch, share news, and eat a lot of candy. It was a small act, and yet we could have been running electricity in ten houses to watch this. And instead, we shared resources, built deep relationships, and had good old silly fun.

Yes, we gave up some convenience, but we gained relationships. And put a little less demand on the earth.

CRISIS HELD IN COMMUNITY

It's been thirteen years and generations of chickens since those early days. Now my kids carry around the chickens and give them ridiculous names. Some folks have come and gone, but many of us are still here. I am so thankful for those early days. We had no idea the ways we were preparing for what was to come.

In March of 2020, when the pandemic first hit and the shelter in place orders came down, we all tucked away in our own houses carrying unbelievable anxiety, exhaustion, and loneliness. We feared for one another's lives. We quickly realized this wasn't sustainable and we needed one another.

So the invitation went out. We began to gather every day at five o'clock. Outdoors. Masked. Distanced. We waved to one another and asked one another how we were doing. We sang together and did sidewalk chalk. We carried on for weeks and then months . . . we sang birthday greetings, beat a drum each day, and threw distanced parades on holidays.

My niece Mabel turned one that April when everything felt the most terrifying. Inside our house I had a branch from our apricot tree covered in flowers to which I had started tying pieces of paper with the names of folks we knew who had Covid. The list of names was growing too long. We were scared. Yet, there we stood. Twenty or so gathered, bringing our own treats, wearing masks, standing ridiculously far away from one another, and singing in thanksgiving for Mabel's life. We found joy.

A couple weeks later at one of the evening gatherings, Cedar learned to ride his bike without training wheels. He raced down the bumpy sidewalk with a huge smile on his face as folks shouted with excitement and applause.

As the days turned into weeks and then months, we continued to check in on elders and those who were immune-compromised. We shared recipes and gathered medicinal plants in our neighborhood to make immune-boosting medicines. We made and shared fire cider. We collected and redistributed stimulus checks to those who were systematically denied relief due to immigration status. We were one another's first line of defense. It was time to care for one another's spirits and bodies.

PREPARE FOR ONE

This was not the first crisis we faced as a neighborhood, and it will not be the last. Little did we know that for so many years, the ordinary ways we showed up as neighbors had prepared us for the pandemic. We instinctively knew how to be there for one another because we had practiced.

Civil rights historian Vincent Harding said, "You can't start a movement, you can only prepare for one."[1] We had put our hands in the dirt, fallen in love with the people and place, and laid the stones, so that one day we would be ready.

The crises faced during the pandemic may not be all that different from what we will face with climate crisis. We may be stuck at home, isolated, without access to the usual conveniences. We may ask similar questions: Can we grow food? Bake bread? Gather medicine? Share resources? Know one another's needs? Find joy in the midst of pain?

Every ordinary act of building community becomes part of the strength we have when disaster comes. There is beautiful simplicity and power in the slow work of learning one another's names, sharing a cup of sugar, sitting on the porch, and telling stories.

COMMUNITY CHANGES EVERYTHING

And beyond the realization that we need one another, community is also an antidote to despair. These are times that work their way into our guts and leave us depressed and uncertain. And yet, it is a lot harder to be hopeless when you are surrounded by loved ones who squeal with joy at a first bike ride, delight at the tickling of baby chicks' little claws, and sing long into the night.

Perhaps most hopeful of all is that there are a million and two ways to build community. There is nothing too small or too big. Small moves to find ourselves some people can make all the difference. I am so grateful for those two kids who wandered into our backyard all those years ago. Hard to believe that one has just finished her first year of college and the other is about to become a senior in high school. I love them. And I am so grateful they love me.

Climate change is going to put the American dream concept of individualism to the test. We have been manipulated into believing that if we are succeeding, then we can handle this on our own. We cannot do this alone. Our hearts will not be able to stand it. And our bodies won't know how to do what needs to be done. We can each learn a little bit and rely on one another for the rest.

LAYING HANDS ON OUR CHILDREN

Same thing is true of parenting. I am so incredibly grateful we are not responsible for teaching our kids everything. There are lots of grown-ups who will weave through their lives, teaching them a million things I don't know.

On our little block nestled between the freeway and truck traffic on Michigan Avenue, there are grown-ups who know remarkable skills that daily give life to our community. I want to surround our kids with folks ready to pour out knowledge and creativity on children. Adults who will swoop them up and take them along on the job. Already my kids disappear with neighbors, learning to build tree houses, catch fish, and play piano. With honey dripping from their chins and down their shirts, they are learning to tend beehives. They are learning how to play soccer and how to make puppets that squirt water from their mouths. Another neighbor rings the doorbell to pull them outside when the warblers and oriole are passing through on their migratory journeys.

And this is just the beginning; as they grow older and follow their hearts' desires, there are neighbors who could teach them to bake bread, speak Spanish, mend pipes, clean chimneys, harvest medicinal herbs, play guitar, throw clay bowls, play chess, make tamales, put up a roof, build furniture, play horns, knit sweaters, cut hair, and on and on and on.

My heart pours out with undeniable gratitude.

We all know how to do something. We don't have to do it all. We can lean on another. We can keep learning new things.

WELCOMING IT ALL

Community can be messy. There is no promise or even possibility of perfection. We humans make mistakes and hurt one another over and over again. In fact, community can be a pain in the ass. But it also has a tendency to save us. I am staking my life on it. And I believe it is the greatest gift I can give to my kids who are walking into the unknown. They will be known and in relationship with others who will be able to hold this work and imagine the way forward. What more could I ask for?

> So dear friends,
> depend on relationships
> over corporations,
> people over technology.
> Need people
> over independence.
> Celebrate that which
> you cannot do alone.
> Why would you want to?
> Pay attention to the needs of others.
> Delight in the skills others have
> that you never will.
> Shower your children
> with community
> and all its love, time,
> mess, and learning.
> In all that you do,
> widen the
> beloved circle.

A BLESSING FOR COMMUNITY

> May the preparation be sweet.
> May the stories,
> and laughter,
> and meals,

be the joy
that can hold you
when the time comes
and crisis falls from the sky.
May each moment
have made you ready
to hold one another.

5 | SEARCHING FOR THE SACRED

"Ooo, hello." Erinn flinched and then cried out for the boys to come and see.

They ran over from across the pond where they had been admiring dozens of toad tadpoles. They slowed their bodies and quieted their voices as they approach Erinn, knowing that there must be a creature to see.

Next to the rock where Erinn sat was a painted turtle with the back of its shell tucked into a hole in the rocky sand.

"It must be going to lay eggs!" exclaimed Cedar.

The kids lay down on the ground just inches away from the turtle and watched as the turtle reached her left hind leg and slowly pulled out a pebble. Then she reached the right leg and pulled out another stone. On and on she worked, minutes disappearing as we watched and marveled at her strength and dedication.

An hour passed. The sun started to set. Isaac was ready to head home. But Cedar wanted to stay. So Erinn took Isaac home, and I searched the car for some old blankets to cover Cedar and me as the night began to chill and the turtle continued her labor.

Time moved slowly. Cedar was alive as he rattled off every fact he knew about turtles.

"I know sea turtle babies use the moonlight to help them find the ocean. Sometimes when humans turn on other lights it confuses the turtles and they end up heading into traffic. We should come back when they hatch and turn off all the lights. We need to clear the beach to make sure there are not any sticks in their way. And protect them from snakes and other creatures that might eat them. How many days 'til the eggs will hatch?"

He was so excited he couldn't stop talking.

We watched the moon rise and listened as the bullfrogs began to sing. We snuggled up in our blankets.

Then, eventually, the turtle stopped digging. She just sat there a minute.

And then she pulled her neck all the way into her shell, lifted her back legs, and we watched as a beautiful white egg slowly popped out, landing in the hole.

Even Cedar had no words in that moment. It was amazing.

And then another egg. And another. Six eggs in total.

Then the slow process of covering up the eggs one pebble at a time. By this time it was so dark we could barely see her. But we knew she was caring for these eggs, as my own baby and I snuggled together under the light of the moon held by the darkness.

As the wind blew across the pond, deep in the brush we heard the crinkling of leaves as animals of the night awoke. There was community there, a festival of friends, a holy circus. That moment of pause and attention was sacred. By sacred I mean one of those moments when time stills and you can feel something move, from the hairs on your arms right to your bones. Something so beautiful and powerful it is hard to articulate, but you know that you have stumbled on something worthy of attention. Whatever it is might nourish your soul or even possibly change you forever. Here beside the pond, under the trees, we honored the life and song and wind and silence as the generations turned. This is the spirit I want my children to know.

These are the sanctuaries that will save us. May our churches not be built of stone, but with walls of trees and ceilings of stars. Let me worship where the chickadee leads the choir and the wild raspberries are in charge of the potluck. Let the streams sermonize and the cedars share the sacred stories. Joining these ancient liturgies can tend and heal our weary souls and remind us what is worth fighting for.

RHYTHMS OF SPIRIT

I know that how we in the dominant culture in United States live doesn't work for my body or spirit. Crops shipped globally have left us disconnected from the shifting seasons. Artificial lights everywhere mean that we no longer depend on the sun. Yet my bones often cry out that something is wrong. I am out of whack. Something else must be possible. A different way . . . one that makes sense in my body.

I long to put my hands in the earth, to feel my body tired from the labor of growing and gathering what I need from the earth to stay alive. I crave a season to be blessed by darkness, to slow down, to eat root vegetables until it is time to emerge to the sweet taste of maple syrup and asparagus. I want my body to feel the pull of the tides and moon. I ache to listen to and echo back the watershed wisdom. I yearn for reciprocity where my body is dependent upon the ground beneath my feet, and that same ground is dependent upon my breath and life.

These changes feel big. They require a whole new way of life. Yet I think it is, in part, the gifts of spirituality that can help get our bodies re-entuned with that earthly rhythm. Each of us define the language, tradition, and boundaries of our own spiritual or religious affinities, yet they offer all of us rhythms that we return to over and over again.

In the Christian and Jewish traditions, it is no surprise that under the liturgical year lies the older indigenous earthly calendar and rituals. The violent brunt of empire has worked tirelessly to steal and conceal the places of wildness in our stories. But those stories are not hard to find if you look carefully and take time, like waiting for a turtle to lay her eggs, as the texts and traditions.

Moments for harvest, death, birth and rebirth, darkness and light, are all built into the rhythms of the year and, therefore, by engaging in the seasonal rituals, they enter into our bodies. Rabbi Arthur Waskow writes about the stories in the Torah like this: "The rain. The dew. The dryness. And then rain again, and dew, and dryness. The story of the circling year. From the rabbis, mystics, and farmers of sixteen centuries ago we have a book that tells the story of the circling year. That teaches us what to do if the delicate machinery should stop."[1]

The machinery has begun to crack. Perhaps some of these old stories can remind us of what we need to do.

For me growing up, the liturgical year is what taught me about justice. I knew the season by where we put our bodies. In Advent, the weeks leading up to Christmas, we would put on our snow pants and mittens and drive out to a weapons manufacturer to stand outside in the snow with candles crying for an end to war. On Good Friday, in early spring, we would walk the streets of Detroit, stopping at places where injustice was happening, mindful that crucifixion continues today. Police stations. Jails. Banks. Schools. Courthouses. The liturgical year offered a rhythm for my body. Year after year, the stories of injustice and the commitment to work against them moved deeper and deeper in my body each time we returned to those places. Now my own children are learning these same traditions.

I think our spiritual rhythms can do something similar when it comes to climate change. Can we welcome back those earthly undertones into our daily practices? Can we imagine a spirituality of strawberries in spring and bonfires in autumn? What are the ecological traditions we return to over and over that will begin to get into our kids' bones? Can climbing up into the apple tree and filling baskets full of fruit not just be a practical act, but a sacred one? And can we invite our children into these routine moments of delight and gratitude?

PRAY OUR WAY

So often prayer can be weaponized. Prayer can be used to exclude and harm folks. It can also be used as an excuse for inaction: *My thoughts and prayers are with you.* There is collective fury at those words every time kids are shot down in a school or there is another mass shooting at a gay night club. F*** your thoughts and prayers! Do something! I echo that anger. And I sure could write a lot about how dangerous and violent institutional Christianity is in these times.

But I also have to admit that I love prayer. I believe it can offer us something transformative.

We cannot pray our way out of climate catastrophe.

However, I believe that prayer can shift how we carry our bodies on this earth. And trust me, when I use the word *prayer*, I mean it in the widest, wildest, most imaginative definition possible. If you say it is prayer, then it is prayer.

Prayer is a container that invites us to bring what we carry. It as an invitational moment that helps us slow down and pay attention to what is right before us. Prayer is also large enough and strong enough not to be afraid of our tears, our rage, our shame, our fear, or our utter exhaustion. And prayer is a place where we can beg the spirit or the universe or God or whoever you cry out to for courage. Prayer is a place to be still long enough to know and commit to the work that stands before us all.

When I think about wanting to pray, it makes me want to turn my heart and body toward the wind and the seed and the songbird. I want to go lie with Isaac and Cedar under a white pine that reaches taller than I can see and marvel at the sun streaming through the branches. I want to run my fingers through a stream listening for water traveling over stones that hold ancient stories. I want to sit with my nieces and nephews admiring and giving thanks for the ants crawling up my feet. I want to rest in silence under a sky full of stars and sing before the crashing waves. I want to listen with the kids in my neighborhood for the wisdom of the cricket and trust the movements of the painted turtle. Left with mud between my toes or snowflakes on my eyelashes, these prayers will soften my shoulders, shift my gaze, and remind me the gift of which I am a part.

And that can change everything.

If I spent more time praying up in a maple tree or lying in beach grass, I would walk differently. I would mourn for losses I had not seen. And I would be forever changed by beauty.

So in these days, let us run toward prayer! Because I believe that if we are truly spending time pouring out our hearts and listening to the wisdom of the ecosystem around us, we will fight in new and more powerful ways. For those of us humans who benefit from a system of capitalism and supremacy, may we let go of our grip on power and money and convenience. And move toward gratitude, reciprocity, and belonging to this earth.

We stand at a crossroads. Either we make dramatic shifts in the systems of power and our lifestyles that will turn from the devastation we have already done, or we are headed for catastrophe and massive death. I fear we may have already chosen our road. Yet both of these paths require our spirits to understand ourselves in intimate relationship with the earth. We will need spiritualities that can help us pour our tears into the soil and stretch the bounds of our imaginations.

If this seems an impossible task, I invite you to call up a toddler in your life, take them into the woods, and follow them wherever they go. Their tottering feet will move slower, and they will spot things you had not seen. They are not afraid of the quiet. And they are no strangers to wonder.

NOT OUR PRAYERS ALONE

As I grab hold of my children's hands and go out searching for the sacred, I realize more and more that our prayers are not alone. This planet holds a multitude of human prayers, honoring the sacred in a billion different ways.

And even beyond those prayers, I trust beyond logic or reason in the mystery and power of the ancestors. Somehow they are encircling us in a cloud. Their prayers for us hold us and love us. As crisis falls, can I cling to the prayers of my mother and my grandmother and my great-grandmothers?

Cedar and I returned again and again to the spot where the painted turtle laid her eggs. Seventy-two to eighty days 'til hatching time, the internet said. We counted the days on the calendar and went back and again and again. We saw no sign of baby turtles or altered stones. Did they not make it? Did they hatch one night and follow the moon into the pond?

I thought of that mama swimming deep under the waters and sometimes sunning herself on the rocks. Was she waiting for them? Was she praying for them? I hoped they found one another in these gentle waters.

Cascading beyond humanity and even beyond the ancestors, is it possible that prayers are also held in the belly of the chipmunk or the cry of the cicada? Does the weeping willow delight in the blessed wind and do the crashing waves hunger for the pull of the moon?

My friend Marcia Lee once took my breath away when she asked me, "How would I live if my life were an answer to the earth's prayers?"

Perhaps even earth herself prays? What if the earth holds her own prayers for me and you and for these children of ours? Prayers tucked in the caves of the coral reefs and in the bark of the grandmother oak? What if she has been praying for millennia? She must hold so much grief, and rage, and hope in her prayers that pour out of her inner being through the trickle of a mountain spring or explode out of a volcano. Her prayers are strong enough to make the earth shake and the rain fall. She knows what she prays for, what she begs for. What if we squandered time trying to listen for the hum of the earth's prayers?

I want my life on this planet to be one answer to her prayers.
And if I live that, how different would my life become?

So dear friends,
find yourself a sit spot, a stone, a tree,
to return to over and over again.
Travel out into the woods with a child
and then part ways to find your own
wild solitude.
Don't be afraid to scream off the mountaintop,
or sing in the wind,
or cry under the willow tree.
Make traditions.
Light that fire at the same moon each year.
Wait to make your favorite soup 'til the first snowfall.
Remember what traditions your parents held,
and your ancestors before them.
Pay attention.
Pick strawberries with reverence.
Cut onions with awe.
Tell your compost heap that one day
you too will become good dirt
to feed the generations
that will come after you are gone.

A BLESSING IN THE WIND

May you hear your name
whispered by the poplar leaves
and feel at home lying in the dark

under a ceiling of constellations.
Hear the earth's prayers
as the winds get stronger,
the rain falls harder,
and the fires rage.
Listen.
Know that even now
she is whispering to you
through the cardinals and the painted turtles
that you are known.
This wild ecosystem
is strong enough
to hold whatever
your heart is carrying.
Let it go. Breathe.
You are loved.

6 | COURAGE TO SPEAK TRUTH

"Are human beings going extinct?"

I lay on the floor reliving the moment when Cedar casually threw out the question. I didn't answer right away. I knew what I needed to say, but I just didn't want to. I wanted to say, "Of course not! You are safe. Everything will be fine!" But I couldn't. I told him I needed to think about how to answer that and that I would come back to it. And I will.

But I needed courage. So I reached over to the cassette player and pressed play. My dad's younger voice came through the speakers. I could almost hear the waves on Lake Michigan and the sound of the engine as he drove through the Upper Peninsula of Michigan.

I was four years old and he had just dropped me at my Grandma Bea's house where I'd stay for three weeks while he, my mom, and my six-month-old sister traveled to the West Bank and Gaza.

They were going with an interfaith human rights delegation to listen to stories on both sides of the occupation. They didn't anticipate experiencing any violence or threat to their lives, but you can make no promises when you enter a war zone. Indeed, there are no promises in anything.

So as my dad left me in his rearview mirror and drove along the sandy shores back toward Detroit, he grabbed a cassette player, pressed record, and left me a love note in his own voice.

"One of the things your teacher told us is that you are a peacemaker. I'm not sure where you learned that. I don't think it was from your mom or me. But she said when your classmates start fighting, you come over and remind everyone that we are friends.

That is one of the reasons that mom and I are going so far away on this trip. Because we are going to a place where people are fighting over things. People whose stories and histories are really the same story, but they are fighting over the land. And sometimes they don't treat one another fairly and they really do hurt one another.

So we are going to go over there. I don't know that we can be peacemakers like you are, but one of the things we want to do is listen for the truth and listen for what would be fair so we can talk about that when we come back.

And we know that that is a little dangerous. Because of the way they are hurting one another and the way they use bombs and bullets and teargas and other things like that. We know that we might even get hurt, but I wanted to tell you that we understand that. I don't think we will, but we might. And we know we might. And that part of helping the people that are being hurt is taking that chance that you might get hurt too. And I don't think there is a way to really help people or understand them or stand with them without taking some of those risks. Taking a chance that we might get hurt.

Maybe you will never listen to this tape. Maybe you won't need to. Maybe we won't need to save it. But just in case, I want you to know how special you are to me. There is no one I love in the world more than you and Lucy and mom.

I remember how stormy the lake was when we walked by the pier yesterday morning. As I drive home, the other end of the peninsula is so calm. Smooth. Like a mirror. Like riding over a sea of glass. I can't wait 'til I see your face again. Lydia, my Lydia. I love you."[1]

My dad had managed to tell me the truth even at my young age. He didn't sugarcoat it. The truth could be dangerous, even deadly. He told me anyway. And through every word of that truth was infinite and unfaltering love for me and for the world.

This was my childhood experience again and again. My parents told us the hard truths of injustice. They found words we could understand and trusted our hearts to hear them. Looking back, I hold nothing but deep gratitude for the unconventional parenting decisions they made in speaking truth to children.

Their truth-telling always felt like an invitation. "Let me tell you of the struggle, dear child. Do you want to join this sacred work?" Their courage to speak with me told me that I mattered; that my showing up mattered, and that my being was strong enough to hold the grief and fear.

TEMPTATIONS

There is a temptation in all of us who love these innocent, beautiful children to keep them shielded from pain for as long as possible. So often, I hear the mantra *Let kids be kids for as long as they can.*

And yes, let kids be kids. Let them play hard. Let their imaginations swirl. Let the world be a place of wonder and delight. But that does not mean we have to shield them from the hard stuff.

You know the beloved children in your lives. You know the intricate and particular ways they process truth. The way it gets digested in their bodies, spun in their minds, and calibrated in their hearts. Trust your gut on how and when to speak. But resist the urge to deny the truth entirely. They won't thank us grown-ups if they wake up at fifteen years old and feel we have lied to them about the dangers and pain inflicted upon their earthly home.

Tell them the truth while they have us around them to love them amid the confusion, grief, and anger. We have the opportunity to let them fall in love with this place while also sharing the imminent dangers that are upon us. Let their hearts break. Let them be angry. Let them fall apart in a place where they are loved. Let the reality around them be part of what forms their hearts and speaks to their future.

Far too often, we believe that we give our kids safety by shielding them from pain. But the truth is that we are not safe. We are not safe from climate collapse, just as so many children are not safe from racism or homophobia or poverty. Safety is a myth.

When I reflect on my own childhood and the radical act of truth-telling I was gifted, I never felt unsafe.

It was not poverty or warfare or climate catastrophe that rocked my sense of security. Safety and security did not come from financial stability, white picket fences hiding what was on the other side, or adults speaking in hushed tones. My safety and security came from feeling totally and completely loved. I was loved for my whole being . . . by my parents and by a wider community. And there is safety in that. I knew I had people I could call on when life got hard.

So, as I lay on that floor holding Cedar's question, I knew that I wanted to speak the truth and wrap my arms around him offering all the love I could muster.

SACRED UNKNOWING

Yet, even if we feel committed to telling them the truth around climate catastrophe, it becomes infinitely more challenging when there is just so much we don't know. Engaging climate change with our kids can feel insurmountable, in part because we don't have the answers. We know their beautiful minds will have endless and powerful questions and yet we have no answers.

It is a parental tendency to not tell our kids something until we know how we are going to say it and what the answers are. This is especially true when it concerns life or death. When it comes to climate change, it just can't be done. We cannot wait for answers. Because we don't know. It is infuriating. It is cause to lie on the floor gasping for breath. But we still won't know.

"What is going to happen?" they ask.

"I don't know."

"How do we fix it?"

"I don't know."
"Will we be OK?"
"I don't know."

"Are humans going extinct?"
"Maybe."

So instead we have to lean into the unknowing. Let that be OK. It is messy. We don't have all the answers. We tell them what we know. And we hold their hand and tell them we are going to figure it out together. It is a time to summon grace and gentleness for ourselves and for our kids. Let's welcome our children into the uncertainty . . . which is a beautiful thing. Those sacred spaces of unknowing may just become fertile ground for our kids' imaginations and hearts.

HEART TRUTH

There is a deep vulnerability in truth-telling and it isn't just words and answers that we can offer our children as gifts of truth. But it is our own hearts as well.

Our children can be blessed by our tears and our anger, our confusion and our shock. I know we don't want to scare them and we have to tread carefully. But expressing our own feelings gives our children permission to explore their own hearts and questions. Through our tender attention and expressions, they will witness that there is a different way than the dominant culture offers. And hopefully, they will know that we can be partners in this journey. We are strong enough for their sorrow. Gentle enough for their screams.

Our kids need to feel the climate destruction they witness. For us to be able to welcome space for their feelings, we have to be able to grieve ourselves. We don't have to be done with it or have moved to some other happier side. We don't have to have all the answers. It doesn't have to look pretty and there isn't any right way to do it. We just have to be willing to face it. Find courage to not look away. And to let what we see alter the fabric of our beings.

Our work in these days, as we love children so abundantly, is to welcome their hearts. We let them cry. We hold them. We resist the parental urge to fix or distract. And we make space for it whenever their grief comes. Because rarely does grief come at a convenient time.

ACHE AGAINST WHAT IS TRUE

I get off the floor and make my way down the stairs and out into the backyard. Cedar is digging in the sandbox.

"Cedar, I don't know the answer to your question about whether human beings are going extinct. So much depends on how we humans choose to live. I hope with everything inside of me that we are not going extinct. But we might be."

What I realized in that moment is that it isn't that I want to hide the truth from my kids. It's that I don't want the truth to be true! I am so angry that we humans have collectively done this to the world. We have done this to our children. I hate the truth right now.

All I can do is go find that sweet kid and share my uncertainty and my anger. And welcome him into the work of living in a way that dares to hope we can change some of these awful truths that stand before us.

And then I have this amazing gift to witness the way the truth metabolizes in their bodies. The ways they shift and pull and are formed into who they are by the world they live in. Each time I witness the ways they engage the aching world, I give thanks for the willingness to speak the truth.

Dear friends,
Let courage find you.
May words come
and tears fall.
May space open wide
for rage and grief.
Welcome the questions.
Bless the unknowns
Hold onto one another
and keep watch for what
is yet to come.

A BLESSING FOR OUR TONGUES

As the questions pour out,
may the silence and uncertainty
lead to collective truth-telling
that opens space
to embrace the fertile, sacred
ground of what can become
when the answer
is "I don't know."
Trust the mystery.

7 | ONE HAND OF RESISTANCE

The snow was still falling while I shoveled our sidewalk. Living on a corner means there is all the more to shovel, but I don't mind. I love the snow. Whenever I could, I would throw my shovel load over to where Isaac was working on an epic fort. We worked in silence. His walls grew as I created a path for neighbors.

Then, out of the quiet he said, "Mommy, I love nature so much. More than anything. I would go to jail for my whole life if it meant that nature could be free and never harmed again."

I put down the shovel and held the silence for a while. So much in so few words. Grief. Longing. A desire to do something.

When your kids say something like that, part of you worries about them—for how much grief they are holding, for how extreme it all sounds. But on the other hand, here he was expressing just how much he loved this world and he made clear he was willing to risk a lot.

WATER IS A HUMAN RIGHT

Even at such a young age, Isaac was no stranger to the idea of taking risks for what you believe in or civil disobedience.

When Isaac was eighteen months old, I watched his eyes widen with attention as water was poured into a ceramic bowl by two elders in our community. This water had been gathered from the Detroit River before dawn. The sun was now starting to rise, but not yet visible over the buildings around us.

We passed the bowl of water around the circle of about twenty-five people gathered in the driveway of the Homrich Demolition Company. We each touched the water with our hands, giving thanks for this river that keeps flowing and literally keeps us all alive.

The bowl ended with my dad, who took it and poured it out in a line all the way across the driveway. Isaac squirmed out of my arms and followed his grandpa along the water path that would soon become a line of bodies.

Homrich had been contracted by the city to turn off water to anyone in Detroit who was $150 or two months behind on their water bill. Thousands of homes had already been shut off and they had orders for 150,000 more homes in the city. No running water in a city where 40 percent of households are living below the federal poverty line. Water is needed for safe drinking, for bathing, for sanitation, for cooking, for laundry. If water is not a human right, what is? And of course, having your water turned off was grounds for the state to remove children from their parents. Detroiters were experiencing an epic crisis.

Water is the heart of the conflict these days from Detroit to California to Palestine. As the climate crisis intensifies, clean water is disappearing. We were standing at one of the fronts of the fight against water becoming privatized.

So on this morning, folks gathered at Homrich, poured water, and blocked the driveway, refusing to let the water shutoff trucks leave the parking lot. For seven hours in the heat, we stopped those trucks from getting to work until the police arrested seven folks.

Over the course of those hours, I followed Isaac around as he waddled through the crowd. Folks would bend down to play peek-a-boo. Isaac joined in dancing when we sang and would raise his fist as folks chanted *Water is a human right!* I put him on my back in a pack for a nap. We ate snacks. It was ordinary and powerful.

After seven hours, we watched as his grandpa and grandma were handcuffed and escorted to the police car. Isaac put his hand up to the police car window and waved goodbye. We would follow behind and wait to bail them out of jail a few miles away.

There was a police officer who had moved through the crowd that day whispering in folks' ears that I was a bad mom for having my kid here. But I can tell you, without a doubt, there is no place I would rather have brought my kid than to witness elders put their bodies at risk out of a love for community and for this city. As words were not yet forming from his tongue, I trust Isaac's conscience was stirring, his understanding of justice growing, and his ability to see that standing up and saying *no* is possible.

STANDING IN THE TENSION

As the climate crisis intensifies and the systems around us continue to perpetuate harm to humanity and all the earth, I believe we must hold the tension of creation and resistance. Part of our work must always be to create the world we want to see. We need to say yes with our whole bodies to what is good and just and creative. We need to try new things and old ways. And yet, on the other hand, we need to keep taking our bodies to the places of injustice (wherever those may be) and crying out a loud and collective *no*.

Resistance is part of naming and exposing that this crisis is not a matter of individuals changing their lifestyles, but that we are battling systemic powers on so many fronts. Corporations. Banks. Government. Schools. Agriculture. Prisons. Religion. All of these systems (and more) are entwined in the destruction of our planet.

I believe there are tremendous gifts to our souls in showing up in the streets and joining with community in resistance, protest, and civil disobedience. And that showing up prods our children's ethics, sense of power, and encourages their voice.

Protest is also one of the beautiful places where we see intersectionality. We realize that all our struggles are bound up together. We cannot talk about climate crisis without talking about racial justice and economic justice. We cannot confront climate disaster without talking about Christian nationalism or patriarchy. We are bound up in one struggle for justice. When folks flow into the streets, you can feel the many threads of liberation.

HISTORY REPEATS ITSELF

In 2018, the Poor People's Campaign organized six weeks of protests that included civil disobedience at state capitols around the country. I spent those weeks organizing at the capitol in Lansing, Michigan. Cedar, two at the time, was my companion. He would pass around the mic at the morning nonviolence trainings. He was an expert at drawing over the carefully plotted maps with direct action plans (unconsciously covering up any trace or possibility of conspiracy charges). He would distribute water under the beating sun to folks blocking doors. When things got tense and I needed to be ready to move, I would strap him to my back. And often he would fall asleep ushered into dreams by the singing strands of *Somebody's hurting my people, and we won't be silent anymore.*

I too had similar lullabies sung to me in bed and on the streets. As a child, I learned the geographical and political land-scape of this place by walking these same trodden streets with signs or songs or snacks. I was first carried upon them in utero, then stroller, then my own feet. And then one day, I carried my own boys in utero and then pushed their strollers. Now I pack helmets and bicycles.

Thirty years ago, my mom held me up to the police car to wave goodbye to my dad and now I lift my own children to the window to wave goodbye to grandpa. I have watched my dad get arrested dozens of times. I've bailed him out. I've sat in court rooms. I've kept vigil outside jail cells as a child and again as an adult.

He is always just one of a communal ragtag team of orga-nizers, storytellers, dancers, medics, drummers, musicians, artists, legal observers, marchers, and deep listeners. A chorus of voices coming together to create poetry, to create protest in an even larger movement for justice.

It is always the same streets, the same buildings, and while the struggles and chants may shift with time, ultimately it is the same struggle. The weight of my feet upon this pavement has been my education, my spiritual formation, and my commitment to this community and place that I love.

PARENTED ON THE PICKET LINE

My parents made an intentional choice when I was born to say that having kids was not a reason to flee from the risks of resistance. Instead, they welcomed us deeply and lovingly into that struggle.

When I was in third grade, there was a newspaper strike happening in Detroit. My parents pulled us out of school every Thursday morning to join the protests. My sister and I were found making up chants and drawing protest signs. It was in those early mornings, playing hooky from school, that we learned that showing up for our community and understanding local struggles was just as much a part of our education as sitting at a desk. And we were learning that our beings, voices, and presences as children mattered.

Resistance in the street is not the whole of the work. Justice must be demanded, built, and created from every angle, drawing on the skills of many from the streets to the neighborhood community centers, from the court room to the sanctuary, from the classroom to the front porch, from the halls of power to the encampment beside the freeway. The work is long and wide, but when thousands (or even just a few) begin to sing in the street, that sound reverberates through your very core. The power of community is palpable. Those moments give us courage and strength for the coming days.

When my mind begins to grow numb and my heart starts to drift toward despair, this is the medicine I need. I move my body into the streets with a community and sing. To cry out for a better way. To say no with everything I've got! There is always a moment for me when the song or the chant gets stuck in my throat and turns to tears. I cannot be in a crowd without feeling my heart give way to hope.

I LOVE EGGS

As we continue to face down the climate change road, some news may be hopeful, but more likely, most of it will be devastating. Systems of power will continue to choose profit over the preservation of the planet. On one hand, we will create alternatives in our local communities. But on the other hand, we must always be paying attention, refusing to turn away, and using our bodies to expose the truth. We must continue to cry out that sacred *no*!

I love that so much of my work as a parent of these two beautiful children is to nurture their consciences and beings as they navigate their place in the ecosystem of what it means to be human. We have a wall along our stairway entrance covered by their protest signs held up with masking tape. Through crayon and marker, I am already seeing their voices grow and shift. One of Isaac's earliest signs reads "Honk for Donald Trump to Be Nice!" I still delight in a sign Cedar drew with abundant color a few years ago. It simply says "I Love Eggs." My work is to honor their voices, trust what they have to say, and welcome them into the great and ancient community of prophetic protest.

Sometimes the best work I can do is pack snacks and mittens and diapers, only to arrive thirty minutes late to a forty-five-minute vigil. Yet, we keep showing up. We bring our bodies and our hearts. We stand as witness. We stand as a reminder that we are not alone.

I want my kids to know struggle, to feel the power of community, to be white bodies fighting for racial and environmental justice, to be washed over by one another's courage and imagination, to be nourished by the joy alive when the masses cry out for liberation. So that when they go home, justice flows into the rest of the day and the rest of the work now and always.

So dear friends,
take the next step.
Find the protest.
Read the newspaper.
Take risks.
Get out those large permanent markers,
posterboard,
write your message.
Trust your voice.
Show up when
young folks
or your elders call
for masses in the streets.
Don't be afraid.
Bring your kids.
Let the song
reverberate
through your bones
and into the rivers.

A BLESSING OF RESISTANCE

Resistance is an old story.
One that formed you and loved you
before you were born.

Generations cried out
knowing you were coming.
Now here you are.
Honor that story into your life
knowing that new generations are coming.
Love those children
with your body,
with your risks,
with your song.

8 | ON THE OTHER HAND, CREATION

When I was eleven, I remember waking up to the sound of sirens. I climbed down from my bunk bed and followed the sounds out our back door. I stood beside my parents watching as our garage went up in flames. It was the third garage that was set on fire on our block that spring.

I watched as the flames rose high in the air. Batteries exploded in a shower of green sparks. Our beloved apple tree wilted under the heat. This tree had moved with us to that house after being planted in memory of a sibling of mine who had died in a miscarriage ten years earlier.

As the fire hoses worked to control the fire, I said aloud to my parents, "Can we put a basketball court there?"

They laughed. I knew it was the kind of comment a kid could make that could just annoy adults as they panicked in a crisis. So I was glad that instead it had done what I hoped and made them smile.

And in a few short weeks, after we had hauled out burnt boards and swept the ash away, we bought a basketball hoop to put on the old cement floor.

We played many years of basketball on that court beside the apple tree that continues to bear fruit each year while still showing signs of the trauma of that fire.

VISION FROM WITHIN THE FLAMES

While I admit this story feels a bit trivial in the face of climate crisis, it reminds me of Grace Boggs who is a beloved movement ancestor in Detroit. She wrote, "Every crisis, actual or impending, needs to be viewed as an opportunity to bring about profound changes in our society. Going beyond protest organizing, visionary organizing begins by creating images and stories of the future that help us imagine and create alternatives to the existing system."[1]

Is it possible that each fire, flood, heat wave, each particular or impending crisis, could actually be an opportunity for imagination and transformation?

What do we see in this crisis? How can we learn? Shift? Can we look at this moment beyond despair into beautiful possibility? Have we been gifted with a moment to lean into being more human? Can these series of crises beg of us to become more alive? What if we could shift away from all that causes violent destruction on this sweet earth and instead let ourselves become creatures of reciprocity? Perhaps, just perhaps, we have a chance to create something new and wonderful!

John Lewis, political and civil rights activist and another among the Cloud of Witnesses, talked about his work in the civil rights movement and the need to "live as if."[2] Live as if the Beloved Community was already here. John Lewis wrote: "You live as if you're already there, that you're already in that community, part of that sense of one family, one house. If you visualize it, if you can even have faith that it's there, for you it is already there."

To "live as if" requires a radical amount of imagination to be able to envision with clarity and beauty that which we dream of being a reality. Summoning such images and stories, amid fear and anxiety and grief, is a muscle that needs to be exercised and tended to.

LIVE AS IF

We don't know what is yet to come. We may be somersaulting into disaster and death and ultimately extinction. But what if we aren't? What if we get it right? What if we wake up and make big changes?

So perhaps, against all better judgment, we do the impossibly hopeful work of "living the if."

What if we decide we don't need so much stuff and we all choose to live with less?

What if we create local communities and economies that release the weight and dependence on oil, technology, and Amazon?

What if we live more seasonally and rest more in the darker seasons and grow food in the summer?

What if we stop creating toxic waste?

What if the ice comes back and the temperatures decrease?

What if we understand the struggles for racial, economic, and climate justice as one fight and create policies that allow all of creation to thrive?

What if we plant more trees and eat less meat?

What if we live in ways that depend less on the grid and the internet and the utilities?

What if we understand ourselves as creatures in this ecosystem in which we live?

You know what I would love to do? Build a composting toilet with Isaac. Lie with Cedar in a field of wildflowers under a solar array. Knit my whole family sweaters. Multiply the canned goods in our kitchen. Build an herb spiral. Put a rain catchment system off every gutter. Hang clothes on the clothesline. Follow the chickens around the yard. Depend on my neighbors. Keep money as local as possible. Work less for money. Depend on the ecosystem where I live for survival. Let the actions of my body not be an extraction on this earth, but a gift to her future.

I want to run toward all that is wonderful! I hunger for these endless possibilities. I long for us all to live into these visions until there is no choice but for them to be made real.

SAYING YES AND SAYING NO

Grace Boggs goes on to say,

"My hope is that as more and different layers of the American people are subjected to economic and political strains and as recurrent disasters force us to recognize our role in begetting these disasters, a growing number of Americans will begin to recognize that we are at one of those great turning points in history. Both for our livelihood and for our humanity we need to see progress not in terms of 'having more' but in terms of growing our souls by creating community, mutual self-sufficiency, and cooperative relations with one another.

Living at the margins of the postindustrial capitalist order, we in Detroit are faced with a stark choice of how to devote ourselves to struggle. Should we strain to squeeze the last drops of life out of a failing, deteriorating, and unjust system? Or should we instead devote our creative and collective energies towards envisioning and building a radically different form of living?

This is what revolutions are about. They are about creating a new society in the places and spaces left vacant by the disintegration of the old; about evolving to a higher Humanity, not higher buildings; about Love of one another and of the Earth, not Hate; About Hope, not Despair; about saying YES to Life and NO to War; about becoming the change we want to see in the world."[3]

This is our work. To live in the tension of holding out both hands. One hand of resistance and one hand of creation. We say yes with everything we've got to all that is beautiful and possible. And we say no with our whole bodies to that which is destroying the earth.

. So we plant tomatoes and draw protest signs. We stop using plastic and we write to Congress. We bake bread and we boycott oil companies. We ride our bikes and we show up in the streets. We fall in love with the chickadee and we get arrested.

Boggs's husband Jimmy said that "Revolutions are made out of love for people and for place."[4] If we love our neighbors and fall head over heels for the oak trees and the wild raspberries, then we will build a revolution.

We say yes with our whole hearts because the vision of what is possible is breathtakingly beautiful. And we say no with everything we've got because our bodies demand it. We are not resisting because we will win or get it right or things will change, but because we cannot not resist. The destruction of this planet does not feel right in our bodies. And we are not living the yes because it will become reality, but because it is demanded of our souls if we are going to live humanly.

THE ARTISTS AND THE GARDENERS

And again, Grace writes,

> "Our responsibility, at this watershed in our history, is to face the past honestly and do the things necessary to heal ourselves and our planet. Healing our society will require the patient work not primarily of politicians but of artists, ministers, gardeners, workers, families, women, and communities. It will require new forms of governance, work, and education that are much more participatory and democratic than those collapsing all around us. It will require enlarging our vision and decolonizing our imaginations."[5]

This crisis is not going to be solved in the halls of power. We cannot wait for climate legislation. The destruction of the planet is too profitable to allow corporations to lead the way.

In Grace Boggs's words, we need the artists and the ministers, the gardens and the workers, the families and communities. We need dreamers and painters, poets and bushcraft survivalists, woodworkers and novelists, quilters and puppeteers.

Every act of imagination and creation is an act of hope. We make beauty and summon ourselves back into our bodies and away from dependence on the powers that be. We can stop buying their myths of scarcity and wealth. Instead, let our lives be an act of subversion by practicing for what we hope is yet to come.

This is how I would want to live. The way. The skills. The joy. The beauty. The creation. Even if we are headed towards total collapse.

We cannot survive this next phase of human history without beauty and imagination. So go out in search of it. Make it with your hands. Let all that is practical be filled with gift and delight. Tend to your souls. Don't be afraid to be obsessed with creation or squander time away on the smallest details. Reject perfection. Demand that our work be filled with art, craft, and imagination . . . in truth it always has.

POCKETS OF JOY

Last year when the first snow began to fall, Erinn and I could be found most evenings curled up by our woodstove with crochet hooks and knitting needles in hand. One loop at a time, Erinn transformed rainbow strands of yarn into an apron with a dozen tiny pockets in front.

On Christmas morning, Cedar unwrapped the apron and shrieked in delight, "For eggs!" Cedar had an unusual affinity for eggs since before he could talk. He loved gathering eggs from our chicken coop each day. Some days we would have to be careful that the eggs didn't go rotten because there were always at least one or two eggs for which Cedar would say, "We cannot eat this one. It is too beautiful."

He asked us to help tie the apron around his waist and he ran out the back door to fill each pocket with an egg from his beloved chickens.

This is the world I can say yes to. This is the world I want to be real. When crisis comes, I'll be grateful that there will be aprons full of eggs.

Dear friends,
exercise your imagination.
Make a daily practice.
Dare to imagine a future
so abundant
so lush
so just
that your soul cries
out for it.
And then live as if
that world were right before us.
Embrace the foolishness.
Let the holy fool
turn this world upside down.

A BLESSING FOR HOPE

May the grief not have run so deep,
or the despair pulled too tight
that you cannot find glimpses of hope.
Grab them when they appear.

Rock them in your arms.
Let them grow
and take on a life.
Follow that hope
wherever she goes.
Live into the beauty she calls forth
despite knowing all the facts.

9 | TOUCHING DEATH

"It's OK to go slow," Cedar whispered as his five-year-old feet stepped gently on the pine-needle-covered trail. "That way you can see more things."

The sunshine wound its way through the branches, lovingly releasing the final patches of snow back to the wet earth. After the long winter months, it is not just the dirt that's exposed, but the stories of what has passed in the woods.

Cedar was searching for these stories. His eyes moved from tangled roots to streambed, taking it all in.

All at once, he cried out for me from behind a fallen ash tree. A rib bone! He sat down and started shuffling through rotting leaves. The spine, a jaw . . . a tooth! What was this creature? he wondered aloud. A fox? A raccoon? How did it die?

Cedar picked up the bones. He ran his fingers along their smooth edges as if he had never seen anything so beautiful. And then he began to fill his pockets. These bones would join the many other bones in baskets beside his bed.

A little farther along the path, we found a long beak at the edge of the stream. It was light and delicate. And longer than my hand! A heron? Once our questions and imaginings had finished, it was time to return to the trail, but Cedar's pockets were already full. He looked to my empty, larger pockets for help. I can't deny it took me a bit of time to willingly lend my hands and pockets for the physical decay and memory of death. But Cedar's requests were persistent.

He skipped ahead, humming with delight. I couldn't help but look at Cedar with awe for his ability to see death in these woods. He didn't appear surprised or shocked by the existence of death and he wasn't afraid to touch it. As we walked, he chattered on about the animals. There was an intimacy in his voice that harkened toward friendship with this creaturely ecosystem. In that moment, I realized he was teaching me to resist a culture that can't look at death. Perhaps I, too, could walk with bones.

As we made our way up the hill, I wondered what bones this kid would touch as he grows older. One day I presume (or hope) that he will bury my own bones. But as I looked out into his future that will be so marked by climate catastrophe, I fear there will be too much . . . too many piles of bones.

CLIMATE CHANGE BRINGS DEATH

So much of what our children are walking into is unpredictable. Just how bad? Are we headed toward human extinction? In how many generations? We don't know. But one thing is certain: They will face more and more death . . . of species, ecosystems, and indeed a growing number of human beings. Floods. Fires. Hurricanes. Earthquakes. Pandemics.

It already surrounds us. A few miles from my house, Marathon oil refinery leaves astronomical cancer rates in the neighborhood. A few miles the other direction, kids' lungs are filled with asthma due to years of the incinerator burning our trash. Environmental racism and climate change reek of murder. For decades, that is the choice we have been making . . . profit over life on this planet.

And yet, in the United States, our culture is repulsed by death and we struggle to weep. We don't remember how to tend to bodies or sit with the dying. We have done what we do best: We have privatized death work. Instead of older loved ones dying in our homes, we send them to retirement and nursing homes. Instead of preparing their bodies for burial in our parlors, we send them to funeral homes. We have an industry that takes care of death, offering us space to look away and not touch it.

We are actively forgetting our ancestral traditions. Forgetting our songs and our rituals, our private grief and our collective mourning, our memory and our posture.

And I'm more likely to forget these things because of how my body sits in this world. Whiteness has everything to do with forgetting. Forgetting history. Forgetting from where we come. Forgetting the skills of our hands. Forgetting the actions of the past for which we are accountable. Forgetting our culture. Ritual around death is just one more piece of forgetting.

REMEMBERING IN A CULTURE OF FORGETFULNESS

Part of our work in this moment must be remembering how to walk with death.

For Erinn and me, part of our work has been to step into our family histories, recovering the rituals and stories that have been lost. This remembering becomes a piece of the web of resistance against racial injustice, capitalism, and climate change.

One of the gifts we have stumbled upon in our learning is the Celtic tradition of Samhain (pronounced SOW-inn). It is marked around November 1 as the time when the veil between the living and the dead is thin. It is a community harvest fire celebration that includes lots of wonderful lore about spirits returning from the dead and great acts of mischief.

But one of our favorite pieces of the tradition is that, at the end of the night, folks carry home a coal from the bonfire. They light their home hearth from the community fire. The hot coal is carried home in a hollowed-out guard or turnip (hence our jack-o'-lantern tradition).

Since our kids were babies, we have summoned friends and family to a bonfire to share stories, drinks, and songs about beloveds who have crossed over. We listen and carve gourds. And at the end of the night, everyone carries home a coal to light fires or candles in their own homes. We always try to hold out 'til that night to light our first fire in our woodstove. The warmth of the winter fire begins holding the stories of ancestors and the love of community.

This past year, our kids couldn't wait for Samhain! I imagined they would stay for the beginning and then their wildness would lead me to shuffle them off to bed. But they stayed to the bitter end, never ceasing from sacred silence and holy listening.

Isaac listened while sitting on a stump with knife and spoon carving out one gourd after another. Cedar sat beside me and sang with me the songs that make me miss my mom the most.

This year, we added a new tradition. With buckets of wood shavings from Erinn's spoon carving, we threw in a handful each time we remembered someone who had crossed over. Cedar's eyes widened in awe as the flames burst higher. Suddenly he was telling stories and calling out names of great-grandparents and soup kitchen guests and beloved pet rabbits and the neighborhood opossum and every last lost chicken. The flames grew higher and higher.

He was learning to remember.

DISSONANCE IN OUR BODIES

"Mommy, why don't people care about the trees?"

I looked up from the road ahead over to Isaac on the bike beside me. He had tears in his eyes. We had just ridden past an area in the woods that was being cleared for development. Trees lay uprooted and scattered on the ground.

"I don't know, my love," was all I could muster. I let his tears wash through my veins, reckoning with the fact that for me the decimation of these trees had just been another in a long line I'd seen before, barely noticeable. Sometimes his tender heart reminds me of all the places I've become numb. Numb because I need to keep going. Numb because it's too much. Numb because if I let tears well up in my eyes, then they will fall and fall and fall and I won't be able to stop.

"Why would people do that? Don't they know we need trees to survive?" his questions continue. Isaac held that grief in his eyes and I watched him. I could tell that it just didn't make sense in his body. How could people just not care?

I remember that feeling of dissonance in my own body. Years ago, I sat on the couch my sophomore year of high school watching TV. I held onto my mom's hand, three years into her battle with brain cancer. We sat together and watched bombs fall on Baghdad. "Shock and awe," they said. It didn't make sense in my body.

My mom had been diagnosed with brain cancer when I was twelve. She was given less than a year to live. While she survived longer, it was a constant roller coaster of surgeries and seizures. Was she living or was she dying?

I had been teetering between the shadow of death and the miracle of life for years now. I knew the grief of a community for a single human being. Her dying reverberated to loved ones all over the world. There was so much grief . . . for one life. Walking with my mom in her dying had awakened me to the gift of being alive. It was then that I learned to pay attention and hold onto gratitude. I valued every second.

And I watched as bombs, paid for and sent by *us*, were killing hundreds and soon thousands of human beings. I had understood nonviolence in my head, but that was the day I knew it in my bones. Grief changed me. I never wanted to lose that sense of dissonance and I don't want Isaac to, either. Yes, my child, it doesn't make sense. It is not OK. Never get used to it. And let the tears you are carrying change you.

The powers that be are happy to fan the flames of dissonance. Look away from the bombs. Look away from the fallen trees so you can keep logging hours. Look away so you can find a happier life on screen. Look away so you won't notice when next time it isn't just a few trees cleared to build a house, but a forest to a build pipeline. Look away so you grow tired and anxious that you lose the will to fight. Look away so you begin to think you are alone and hope starts to feel impossible.

In a culture designed for flashing lights and instant gratification, grief becomes resistance. A refusal to look away. Weeping and raging offers a cultural paradigm shift.

We need to let ourselves weep. Alone. In community. With our children.

I wonder how we would all be changed if we spent more time mourning together. I think we are hungry for it. I know I am. What would happen if we made space to grieve with our kids when a loved one or beloved pet dies? What if we paused to mourn the baby robin on the sidewalk or the garden beds at the end of fall? Perhaps, while holding that grief, the personal and political decisions that destroy the climate might not be as easy to stomach.

BACKYARD FUNERALS

I want our kids to be able to notice death, to look it in the eye, and to sit in witness. I want them to be able to hold dying bodies in their arms. I want them to know how to pick up a shovel, dig a hole, and feel the dirt under their fingernails. I want them to be able to utter prayers and songs from memory that tend to grieving hearts. I want them to know how to speak out of tears with gratitude for life. I want them to know the transformative power of public, communal mourning.

So we make space. Sometimes that is as simple as slowing ourselves down enough to let our children feel what is already rising up within them. Sometimes this means turning the car around because they saw a dead fox on the side of the road. It means following them as they move close to examine the body hit by a human moving too fast. It means staring at it a little longer than we are comfortable with.

And we hold a lot of funerals. There is a little patch in our backyard full of weeds and tulips and a few homemade tombstones. In this fertile ground are composted memories of beloved fish, brutally attacked chickens, stray cats, and two beloved rabbits. We can still recall most of their names—Two, Baubee, Three Train, Autumn, Raccoon, and Luna.

Raccoon, our pet bunny, was perhaps the hardest funeral we've held in the backyard. He was a snuggly friend that both boys turned to on their sad days. He died one night when neighbors were setting off fireworks. He was literally scared to death in mid-jump.

We invited lots of family and neighbors over for this one. We dug the hole and collected peonies and columbine. As if death work was in his own bones, Cedar picked up the body and held him like a baby in his arms. He instinctively started around the circle for everyone to say goodbye and touch his furry, lifeless head one last time. We started singing as Cedar placed Raccoon's body in the hole. I sat beside the grave to be at his eye level, worrying about his heart. He immediately fell into my arms crying and pounding on my chest. Grief poured out of him with all the rawness of rage and sadness. And then, prodded by his older brother, he moved that grief into his body and poured handful after handful of dirt into the hole. He watched his beloved bunny disappear forever.

As a mom, I ached for his heart, so tender and full and in pain. But I also held onto that moment knowing that this is what I want for who he is and for his touch upon the world. Everything will try to squash this out of him, from whiteness to maleness to individualism to consumerism. I don't ever want him to lose sight of life or death, of pain or rage, of body or dirt.

BACK TO THE EARTH

Eventually, the baskets of bones beside Cedar's bed get too full. Little by little, we bring a few bones out to our herb garden around the peace pole. We lay the bones in the dirt, knowing that here and now death can become life again. Here the bugs return once more to fill their bellies and worms feast on the nutrients as the bones decay back to dirt. Eventually the bones will become food for the sage and thyme whose roots rest in this place. I will gather up bouquets of herbs, bringing them into my kitchen where then the bones will get inside us. I give thanks for the fox or raccoon we found that day meandering through the woods.

What a miraculous journey. I can only hope that one day my own death will also be transformed into new life in a thousand different ways. Isn't all of creation part of the dance of resurrection? I have feasted on death and delighted in the gifts of life. May I offer my body back as gift.

Dear friends,
feel the invitation
to move slow.
Let your eyes
search for stories
Remember the names
and traditions
of those who have left.
Light the fire.

Raise a glass.
Dig the hole.
Weep.
Give thanks.
Breathe.

A BLESSING FOR NOURISHMENT

May bones
find you
and share their
stories.
May the dreams
of the ancestors
summon you to live.
The land you tread
is holy.
Mixed in the soil
are the tears of the ancestors.
Let this earth nourish you.
And may you bless this place
with your own tears
until it becomes
mud.

10 | WALKING IN GRATITUDE

"Do you mind if I go see my tree before it gets dark?"

Cedar smiles at Erinn's nod and runs off into the woods.

We have just finished our first experiment with Wild Church. It's a chilly day in February. The trees are bare and the ground frozen below our feet. A couple dozen folks have gathered around a roaring fire in a clearing surrounded by forest in hopes of nourishing the soul and experiencing the sacred.

We sing as the sparks fly and the redtail hawk watches from her bare winter's branch. And then we stick pen and paper into our coat pockets and each venture into the woods alone in search of finding a beloved tree. I roam the woods, touching the bark and admiring the roots of trees until I find a tall tree whose roots wrap around a large rock that beckons me to come and sit. We each write love letters to the trees and promise to return again.

It's almost impossible to get our kids to sit quietly in the pews of institutional church. I don't blame them. But it was not hard for them to join the fire or disappear into the woods to find a new friend.

A few minutes after Cedar had disappeared into the woods, he returned and grabbed Erinn's hand. "Do you want to meet my tree?" She followed him into the woods and off the trail to a tree whose trunk was bent over, as if grown just for Cedar's body to curl up upon. He climbed up the trunk, lay down, and wrapped his arms around the tree. Then he looked up at Erinn and asked, "Would you show me your tree?"

GRATITUDE AS RESISTANCE TO GREED

As I began to write this chapter, I started to wonder how this chapter on gratitude was different from the chapter on searching for the sacred. That tells you something about my theology and my posture around prayer.

If I had to choose one guiding value I'd hope for our family, I'd probably say gratitude. Gratitude flows below the surface of everything.

In fact, we've probably drilled it into our kids so much that, in true kid fashion, they are currently resisting it. When we have company over for dinner, we go around the circle and share a gratitude, they are quick to say, "I am grateful that gratitudes are over," or "I am grateful I don't have any gratitudes."

I give them a mom look and roll my eyes, but I know deep down they know how to look at the world with awe and thanksgiving.

When Erinn and I first started dating, we did a year of long distance. I was living at Jonah House, a nuclear resistance community in the tradition of the Catholic Worker in Baltimore, and Erinn was doing Jesuit Volunteer Corps in Hartford.

Just past sunrise one morning, I sat on the couch joining the community for morning prayer. Liz McAlister, a beloved mother of the anti-war movement, reflected that "gratitude is the only resistance to greed."

Starting that day, I began jotting down daily gratitudes and sending them off to Erinn. We quickly began a habit of sending each other 10 things we were grateful for every day. It was beautiful. Little bits of delight and wonder. We learned details of our lives that might not have emerged in a "how are you?" conversation. We paused to give thanks for the smell of the lilacs through the window or a coworker making lunch or a song on the radio or the feeling of cutting sweet potatoes. It changes you. I honestly attribute that practice more than fifteen years ago as being key to the strength of our marriage. We are always on the lookout for gratitude in one another and in the world. And we are quick to name it aloud.

I don't take it for granted. Gratitude is a muscle that I think is rarely exercised in our capitalist culture. We are fed myths that we don't have enough, that what others have is better, that more stuff means happiness. Gratitude declares that it is enough . . . more than enough.

Years ago, I attended a meeting where we were offered a prompt to name a couple of things we were grateful for. And a beloved friend sat awkwardly, unable to come up with one thing. He took so much time sitting and thinking, and in the end had to pass.

And I get it. It is not easy. Life is hard in general. Plus the world is crumbling. We are not making changes fast enough for any real climate resiliency hope. We are in trouble. What does gratitude matter? How can we find energy for it?

Honestly, I think gratitude keeps us alive. Keeps us breathing. Reminds us that even in the crumbling, we are surrounded by beauty and love and goodness. Gratitude does not ignore the pain. Gratitude finds beauty in the cracks of the pain. And it turns out those cracks are long and wide and abundant. We just have to pay attention.

AN INVITATION TO SLOW DOWN

The summer after my freshman year of college, I came home to care for my mom. I didn't know it then, but she would die six months later. She had just gone through another brain surgery and a few weeks in rehab. She was home but needed someone with her at all times. Someone who could continue her occupational and physical therapy with her.

So I spent the summer helping her get dressed, reading out loud, playing some version of Scrabble, and taking long walks in the neighborhood. By long, I don't mean we went very far, but that it took a long time.

Each day we would walk out the door and slowly move down the eight steps to the sidewalk. Each movement took intention and strength. And then we would begin to walk around the two-block neighborhood where I grew up.

Each day, I would hope that we could get her some good exercise as part of her healing. Maybe walk the loop twice. But she always had other plans. We couldn't get ten feet without her stopping to smell the flowers. She would *ooh* and *ahh* at their beauty. She was mesmerized. I would gently grab her arm and try to move her along. But she would not be moved. She would plant her body by those flowers and delight in their beauty for as long as she wanted.

When she would finally start moving again, it wasn't more than 20 feet before we would stumble upon another patch of lilies of the valley or black-eyed susans.

For a while, it drove me crazy. I knew this was the brain cancer. Before her diagnosis, she moved swiftly and surely. She would move with intention and fierceness. Now everything was slow and felt distracted.

It took me a couple of weeks to let go of my impatience and instead receive this gift. Along those long walks, I learned to slow down, to pay attention, to see beauty, and to give thanks. Each time she grabbed my hand and said, "Oh Lydia, isn't this beautiful?" it was an invitation to let go of everything else except the beauty that stood right before me in this little corner of Detroit. I love my mom for this gift and have always tried to hold onto it.

There was one house on the block that was always the hardest to get her to keep moving past. It was right on the corner with a big chain link fence around it. But pouring out through the cracks and over the top were lilac bushes and climbing red roses and flowering fruit trees. It took her breath away. We would stand outside this stranger's house for twenty minutes each day, admiring each petal and smelling each flower.

Six years later, Erinn and I bought that house. We nurtured the lilacs and roses back to life after the yard had been home to six bulldogs for a few years. It became home to our chickens and our babies, to cherry trees and rhubarb plants, tree houses and swing sets. This is the little stretch of dirt where our family put down roots, where we fell in love with the land, and where we offer gratitude each day.

Every now and then, I can still see my mom standing outside the gate, smelling the roses.

A PATCH OF WILDFLOWERS

Over the last decade, we've tended that little yard with native plants and wildflowers. My nephew, Ira, loves learning the names of wildflowers. He would follow me around the yard asking, "What's that called?" again and again. "Columbine."

"Woodruff." "Bleeding Heart." I think he thought I was magical when I knew what they were called. The truth is, he is magic, and one day he will know far more flower names than I do.

One spring at the beginning of the pandemic, when Ira was three, his excitement could not be contained when our yard filled with deep purple violets. I had recently stumbled on a recipe for violet syrup. So the two of us set to work. I sat down on the lawn and he crawled under the apple tree and we picked hundreds and hundreds of violets. Then we sat together and chatted away as we separated the petals from the stems. We put them in a glass jar and covered them with water. The jar sat on the windowsill for a couple days and every few hours he would tiptoe in to watch as the water grew a deeper and deeper purple in the sunlight.

In the end, we used some syrup to make violet jelly and the rest we poured into lemonade. We drank it outside sitting among the violets. And for those few days, I witnessed Ira learn the name of the plant, tend the plant and talk with it, harvest it, and have his body nourished by its goodness. He was falling in love with this little patch of earth to which he belongs. And there is no question that this land loves him right back.

Generations of beloveds keep loving this same stretch of earth and offer gratitude for the beauty in our midst. Amid brain cancer, amid pandemic, amid climate catastrophe, the earth continues to be good earth. Life keeps growing. Flowers keep blooming. Bees keep pollinating. Caterpillars keep building cocoons in the milkweed. Violets shine their purple petals. Roses lift their aroma toward the heavens. It is enough. It is more than enough.

So dear friends,
go out alone into the woods

and find yourself a friend
whose roots are deep
and whose bark feels right
upon your fingertips.
Slow down.
Walk annoyingly slow
through this world.
Smell the roses.
Harvest violets.
See the ancestors' shadows
continue to linger on
these lands.
Amidst the pain and the crumbles,
give thanks.
Again and again.
For it is enough.
It is more than enough.

A BLESSING FOR GRATITUDE

May you walk
the trail of gratitude
leading you deeper
into the forest
of awe and beauty.
For indeed,
gratitude
is the only resistance to
greed.

11 | THE INESCAPABLE CONVERSATION ON TECHNOLOGY

"Ahhhhh!"

Popcorn flew everywhere!

"No!" The kids were yelling with their arms up in exasperation. Erinn and I had just told them that starting tomorrow, we would be doing a digital detox. No screens for two weeks.

I had worried about their reaction; I thought they would lose it. But at first, they just stared at us. We told them how video games and streaming are designed to give you dopamine hits. That you need more and more and it's never enough. It becomes addictive. It takes two weeks to reset your dopamine levels.

We had been researching the consequences of too much screen time on children. Kids struggling with engaging in conversations with grown-ups. Feeling bored if not on a screen. Having a hard time concentrating. We could see some of these signs and wondered if it was personality, developmental age, or a real consequence of screens in their lives.

In a lot of ways, Covid increased their screen time without very much thought. I remember Cedar at four years old navigating a laptop to get on screen with his circle of preschoolers. Ever since that moment, even back in the classrooms, screens seem to be an hourly reality. And then they come home and turn on the TV to relax, and then some days they also play video games.

Video games were now all our kids could think about. They talked about them all the time. They begged for more. And then they would get on and most of the time bicker with one another as they played. We knew we needed a shift. I worried that it was too late. Once you were this far down the rabbit hole with technology, could you pull back? Could our kids find different rhythms? We knew that everything about our values and desires for them meant we wanted to find another way. One that engaged their brains in community, in books, in crafts, in solitude, and with the earth.

Don't get me wrong—screens can be dead useful in parenting. It made it so we could leave the house and run to the backyard for ten minutes or get a load of dishes done or hop on a Zoom call. They were happy and it made everything easier. So there is no judgment here. But we needed to know what life would be like if we turned all the screens off.

So we shared it all with them—the reasons and plan. They took it all in and nodded. They were taking it like champs. It was me that said, "It's OK to be frustrated. It's a big change. You can be mad and throw this popcorn." They laughed and then picked up popcorn and threw it all over the house while screaming in exaggerated despair. Popcorn everywhere. And then we picked up and headed to the craft supply store and the library because we were going to need some supplies to support us through this early boredom.

THE DANGERS BEFORE US

I am no technology expert. And I do not doubt or diminish the extraordinary developments technology has made in our lives and will continue to make. But there are also some dangers I see for our children and for us grown-ups.

The other day Cedar said to me, "When I grow up, I am going to build a factory, that as you make things, turns carbon dioxide into oxygen. So it will actually be good for the earth." What a beautiful desire, and yet I worry that so many of us are hoping technology will somehow save us in the end. We continue to live as if everything is "normal," hoping that some scientists and tech wizards will bail us out of this mess. It becomes a cop-out for doing the real work we need to do on a massive scale if we hope to avoid the worst.

Over seventy-five years ago, we created the nuclear weapon. In that moment, we made a collective decision around the world that we were willing to have the power to destroy the earth. Perhaps it's not that big a jump for a country founded on genocide and slavery. There are now 19,000 nuclear weapons stockpiled in nine countries: the United States, Russia, France, China, the United Kingdom, Pakistan, India, Israel, and North Korea. Ninety-five percent of those belonging to the United States and Russia. The United States has 1,744 nuclear warheads deployed and ready to be activated at any second. If these all go off, it would set the planet into a nuclear winter.[1]

That technological innovation forced humanity to make a decision of conscience. In some circumstances, would it be acceptable to destroy the earth? When we said yes, our DNA changed, shifting how we relate to this earth. If you have already made the decision that it is OK to destroy the earth, then the slow burn of the planet becomes a lot more palatable.

The other danger I see is that technology is pouring trillions of dollars into creating worlds more enticing than the real one before us. There are the worlds of social media so addicting we would rather scroll while eating at a restaurant with friends or sitting on a park bench in the woods. You see it everywhere. Phones out all the time sucking us in.

But there is also so much brilliance and money being poured into creating alternative realities. We are building whole new tech worlds so that when this one no longer becomes livable we can escape into whole new universe. Places that are designed to hold culture and entertainment and be a substitute for embodied community. We are falling in love with different worlds than the one we inhabit.

FALLING IN LOVE WITH A DIFFERENT WORLD

As our kids entered the world of video games, we worked hard to avoid the most violent ones. But I still watched as they began to fall in love with these other worlds. It was consuming. It was certainly joyful, but soon they'd rather be there than with company around the dinner table.

As they built worlds in Minecraft, I heard them share the differences in strength between oak, birch, cherry, and maple. They were learning elements of stone, lava, and bedrock. They named beloved pigs and built houses for chickens. And I watched in astonishment as they opened pixilated craft boxes and turned stone plus cobblestone plus a stick into an ax. Or leather into leather boots. Or string plus sticks into a bow and arrows. Or eggs plus milk plus sugar plus wheat into a cake. They were learning a lot and having a blast.

But I wanted them to know oak trees by the feel of their bark. I wanted them to know what pigs smelled like. And how to pick up a carving knife and stick and make that bow with their own two hands. I wanted them to know the tools of crafting by holding knitting needles in their hands, or spatulas and measuring cups. I wanted them to smell that cake and know the feel of the boots on their feet. I wanted their brains and their joy consumed by the very real world that surrounded them.

DETOX DELIVERED

So we did it. We kept screens off for two whole weeks. No video games. No TV. And that went for Erinn and me too. When we weren't working, we were off screen. We turned the ringer on so we could hear if someone called and then placed the phone on a high shelf in the kitchen not far from where a corded phone might have hung a couple decades ago. We wouldn't miss an emergency, but we would stop scrolling. We would stop being more accessible to work or social media than to the children in the room.

It did require of us more willingness to be available if our kids wanted to spend time together. We crafted together and played board games. We read out loud to them and went on family adventures.

It was amazing. It was such a dramatic shift in our kids that we extended it another two weeks. And then at last we said they could have one hour each on Saturday morning for screens. That was it. Otherwise, screens could be used for researching or for the occasional family movie night.

When that summer began with the digital detox, we made a reading challenge and hung it on the wall. Isaac and Cedar collectively read more than one hundred chapter books and graphic novels that summer. Isaac took up baking, leaving the kitchen constantly a mess, but our bellies delighted in his newfound talent. Cedar's anxiety decreased. They both stopped fighting as much. When they got bored, they went outside and built forts.

Even their hospitality skills and conversations around the dinner table matured. Their dinner etiquette with company still leaves lots to be desired—manners have always been a struggle for them. But the chaos has decreased and they both love engaging in the collective conversation.

We asked the kids how they felt and what they had learned two weeks into the detox.

Isaac said, "We found out what we can do when we aren't on the screen. I liked getting outside more and spending time with family. It works. Other families should try this."

Cedar chimed in, "Now I feel like I would rather go to the pond and check on those toad eggs than play video games. Kind of."

"We haven't gotten crazy or crabby or bored." Isaac said.

Cedar nodded, "We haven't hurt each other at all!"

They were articulating the same changes I had seen in them. And they felt the shift in us, as our phones were less present when we were together. And in reality, I don't love scrolling. I'd much rather have time with my kids.

I am grateful to learn that it is never too late. You can get hooked on screens and realize it's too much and shift. It's never too late or irreversible.

The world we live in is breathtakingly delicious. Along with my kids, I want to fall head over heels for all that I can smell and touch and see and taste and hear. I will not allow my conscience to accept the slow burn. And I will not wait for technology to save us. And I don't want another world besides this one.

Dear friends,
turn off the screens.
Unplug the device.
Look into the eyes of those nearest you.
Run your fingers down the bark of the old oak.
Bake bread.
Resist the acceptance of destruction.
Know that it is not too late
to shift and turn course
in the small and gigantic ways.
Fall in love with
this world
of flesh and bone.

A BLESSING FOR CHANGE

May the screens go dark
making way for the Milky Way
to appear in the sky.
May we tend our conscience
and find hope in community.
May we love the world
and shift now
while the vegetables still grow
and the snow still falls.

12 | TEACH YOUR CHILDREN WELL

"Mommy, it spilled."

I cringed, not wanting to look.

Our house was a disaster.

Scraps of felt and pillow stuffing covered the living room floor. Hot glue was dripping all over the coffee table. And the googly eyes were everywhere!

And the kitchen, you ask? There was flour in crevices I didn't know existed. Apple peels had fallen in the butter dish. And the rolling pin was being pushed around on the floor by the dog.

Isaac had clearly eaten too much sugar in the course of his baking endeavors. And Cedar was sliding across the wood floors, crashing into anything in his path.

Sometimes, as a parent, it is hard to let the chaos reign.

But if I can pause to take a few deep breaths and let the mess sink into the background, I notice that on Cedar's feet are red felt slippers he designed himself, stitched together with hot glue. And tucked in his bed is a freshly crafted family of stuffed animals, each with a name and a story to tell. And resting on the counter, Isaac is admiring his homemade apple-blueberry pie created without a recipe.

These sights and smells ease my worries.

These kids of mine will be OK.

I cannot predict what the future will look as the climate continues to collapse. Nothing feels sure. I don't know what they will face or what particulars they will need as they stumble into this future.

I trust that they will be OK if they are comfortable in the mess and the chaos. I am witnessing their creativity and ability to create with their hands something new out of something old. They can make food that tends not only to their bodies, but also to their spirits. They are keeping an eye out for beauty and can create it with bits of this and bits of that. And, thank God, they can laugh . . . that deep, uncontrollable giggle at an epic crash landing or the site of some well-placed googly eyes.

They will be OK.

A PARADIGM SHIFT IN EDUCATION

As I help my oldest with yet another worksheet sent home from school, I think about how they are still learning in a structure designed to send kids into the industrialized corporate world. Bells were put into hallways to prepare children for factories. Standardized tests continue to be the priority, starting before kids can read to get them ready for college.

But is that really what these kids need? Is it really what our world needs?

We missed such an opportunity during the year(s) when kids didn't go to school during the coronavirus pandemic. The narrative everywhere is how far behind these kids are and how they lost two years of their education.

I don't buy it. These kids survived the tragic and terrifying onslaught of a global pandemic. They learned how to be adaptable. They experienced grief and loss. They had different learning methods with different people. Some experienced being alone and others learned alongside siblings and family. It was unbelievably difficult . . . for some more than others. Their generation has been changed by it. I am eagerly awaiting who this generation grows to be and how these years will have marked them. They have learned skills and lessons that I certainly never understood when I was so young.

And how much more we could have done! School systems worked so hard to keep drilling in multiplication facts and phonics by converting to more technology. Cedar first experienced a laptop by hopping onto his preschool Zoom room. But what if we had thrown it all out and collectively reimagined education? Let kids rest and play and keep elders company. What if they had learned from the localists of communities in their neighborhood? What if we did outdoor story history tours of the places we live? What if we had kids start gardens? What if we had let it be a year for imagination and trying new things?

A STORY OF SEEDS

A couple of summers ago, I was at a writing retreat at Collegeville in Minnesota, where I first began to put some of these words onto the page. On an invitation and a whim, I walked over to St. John's Abbey's pottery studio. As soon as I stepped in the door, I instantly knew I was in a sacred space. Ritual was everywhere as the wheels spun, turning mud into vessel. In the center of the room was a small fire with a teapot hung over it. I was handed a clay mug filled with tea and a freshly baked cookie. Poetry was read. Stories poured out.

In the 1970s, Richard Bresnahan had stumbled upon some clay a few miles down the road that would soon be paved over. He got permission to store it in the woods of St. John's Abbey and organized a crew to dig and carry it there. In a week, they stored eighteen thousand tons of clay that will last the studio three hundred years. They fire all their pieces in a wood kiln that is lit once every three years using wood sustainably harvested from the acres that surround the abbey.

That story alone would have been enough to take my breath away, but at the end of our teatime, Richard gifted us a large book called *Kura: Prophetic Messenger* about his recent art installation. We leafed through the pages as he told us the story.

The *Kura* sits in the heart of campus. It is a cyclical structure about fifteen feet tall. Inside are clay pots, each filled with smaller clay jars. Inside the jars are seeds. One hundred seventy-eight seed jars, each with ten seeds from one hundred eighty-two varieties of the three sisters: corn, squash, and beans. The seeds are all heirloom and were chosen in relationship with the local indigenous peoples. Tucked in each pot with the seeds was the name and history of the seed, as well as the name and story of an artist Richard had worked with who had a lasting impact on his life and the world. Seeds as artists and artists as seeds. Art and Survival.

Resting in this unmarked structure, passed each day by hundreds of students, was enough food carefully preserved to feed this local community. The seeds should be safe in there for hundreds or even thousands of years, waiting for the day when crisis would come, fertile seeds would be gone, and hunger would reign.

After we left the studio, we wandered through campus until we found the *Kura*. I stood before it, feeling the weight of my body on that land. It was enough to make one weep. Enough to beg the question *What is it that we will do with this one life?*

Why isn't this what we are teaching in our schools? Why aren't we learning history, making art, and concretely caring for the generations that will come after us? What if every public school built a *Kura* in their courtyard? How would students be changed if they walked past that every day?

REMEMBERING THE OLD WAYS

While nothing is certain, I feel pretty confident that the skills this generation of kids is going to need have to do with remembering the old ways we have forgotten. We need to revalue the work done by our hands, the work that moves our bodies. They are going to need to know how to grow food, how to preserve it, how to bake bread, how to repair old pants, how to slaughter a chicken, how to fix a plumbing problem, how to make beeswax candles, and so on. And I think they'll need to know how to sit in a circle with folks off screen and find joy. We need to bring back song circles, scary stories, joke-telling, poetry, and fiddling.

So our family does bits and pieces as best we can. We have fruit trees—apple, cherry, apricot, plum, and peach. We can jam and dry herbs. We knit hats and carve spoons. We put seeds in the ground. We heat with a wood stove and chop our own wood fallen from around the neighborhood. We host bonfires for neighbors. We make homemade Christmas gifts. And it is the most delightful fun.

There is not much that is better for the soul than filling a basket with branches of basil and fresh tomatoes. I eat ice cream with one of Erinn's hand-carved wooden spoons. I am a few inches away from finishing my first ever knit sweater for her. Keeping my fingers crossed that it fits. It's all joy. Dirt under my fingernails and calluses on my hand . . . that's the good stuff. That is the stuff that keeps me sane whenever everything feels like stress.

Little by little, we will keep expanding our skills and expanding our community (for again, we do not have to do everything on our own). Slowly but surely, we are finding our way back into our bodies, back in line with the seasons, back to work that is gentler on the earth.

The truth is, even if we somehow manage to avert climate disaster, and the world goes on as "normal," these are still the things I want my kids to know. These are the skills that remind us that we are human. That keep us in touch with our bodies and their relationship to the earth.

I so often hear parents and grandparents cry out with grief that "my kids won't have what I had." Honestly, that's OK with me. Maybe they will have something better! Maybe they will live more humanly, more connected to life and death, and more in relationship to the earth. That's not a bad way to live.

A LITTLE PLOT OF DIRT

In the spring of 2020, as the world shifted all around us, Erinn and I went to our garden beds and began pulling up the young weeds to make room for seeds. We took one garden bed, eight feet by four feet, and put a little garden gate down the middle.

"It's yours," we said to the kids. "Do whatever you want with it."

Isaac and Cedar's eyes lit up. Then they got immediately to work.

Erinn and I worked on the other beds around them, delighting in their diligence and enthusiasm. In the end, their little plots could not have been more different. Their own skills and personalities poured out on that little stretch of dirt.

Isaac placed five sunflower seeds in a circle. Four pepper plants in each corner. A tomato plant in the middle. And then a circle of marigolds between the plants carefully selected and ordered so that they slowly changed colors as they moved around the circle from bright yellow to deep red. I had never seen anything like it. Isaac is an artist and he had made a work of art!

Once the plants were in, he didn't feel much need to check on it or weed it. All plants were welcome in his garden. Yet those sunflower seeds still grew ten feet tall, with incredible flowers at the top. He was never interested in harvesting a thing. He planted those sunflowers and vegetables intentionally for the birds and the squirrels and the bugs. That is who he is, always wanting the creaturely neighbors to be fed.

And Cedar, on the other hand, worked his little plot quite differently. I watched him put in a long row of carrot seeds, a few lettuce starter plants, four bell pepper plants, and one strawberry plant. When he was done, I said, "Tell me about what you planted."

"I planted the carrots and lettuce for Luna (our pet bunny) because she loves carrots and lettuce. The bell peppers for Isaac because he loves peppers. And the strawberry plant for me."

Cedar's garden was an act of noticing and care for those he loved. He came with us every day to that garden to lovingly tend and weed that little stretch of earth. He talked to the plants and adopted the surprise tomato plants that grew from last year's fallen harvest. Every day, he would pick lettuce leaves and pull up a few carrots and take them back to his grateful rabbit.

Erinn and I built these raised beds more than ten years ago in the backyard where I grew up. They've been mended and tended to and cared for by numerous folks in the neighborhood. When we began, we tested the soil only to learn that the dirt was filled with lead. For how many generations have we been poisoning the ground beneath our feet? So we built raised beds and composted our food scraps. Little by little, this dirt is being renourished.

Ten years ago, we never would have imagined these two boys with their hands in the dirt. They are being educated and formed by this soil. And may the very act of tending this earth not only give them skills for what crisis is to come, but also break a cycle of carelessly poisoning the soil, the air, the waters of which we are part.

Dear friends,
question the methods.
Dream new ways.
Reclaim the old skills.
Find the rhythm of the earth
in your body.
Put your hands in the dirt.

Make stuff.
Embrace the mess.
Squander time on beauty.
Trust the artist.
Lean on community
for our common survival.

A BLESSING FOR OUR HANDS

May your fingers know
the crumble of the dirt
or the grain of the wood
or the pull of the yarn
or the smoothness of clay.
May you know your life
dependent on the sun and the moon
and the seed and the song.

13 | THE ANTIDOTE OF JOY

The waves crashed and the kids squealed. I delighted in watching Isaac and Cedar as their bodies found the joy that never seems to grow old from one generation to the next. Following the wave down as the tide pulls the wave out into the Atlantic Ocean, and then screaming in fear and joy as the wave rushes back to chase you—sometimes faster than your legs can carry you.

The kids moved along the shore out toward the point where the lighthouse stood. They played with the waves and combed the beach for treasures. With each crab claw and cracked clam shell, they would run to show us. Our backpacks grew heavy with beach finds.

I held Erinn's hand as we made our way along the ocean shore behind them. I breathed in the smell of salt and fish in this unfamiliar ecosystem that always felt nothing short of magical.

We made our way out to the rocky tip where waves crashed as the tides collided on both sides of the island. It wasn't until we were fifty feet from the edge that Cedar stopped in his tracks and said, "Wait! Those aren't rocks, they are seals!"

Sure enough, we were just feet away from a whole community of seals sunbathing on the shore. We all froze as the enormous gift took our breath away. The four of us moved slowly to a driftwood log and sat, watching. The seals would look over at us with their puppy-dog faces and then turn over. Between these enormous creatures we could see babies resting up against them. They didn't seem scared of us. We all just rested there a long time, watching one another.

After twenty minutes or so, the kids were feeling brave and walked closer to the seals. Erinn's and my anxiety rose as our youngins approached these monstrous creatures. We didn't want to alarm our kids or pass along any fear of animals that wasn't necessary, but we also didn't know the ways of these beautiful seals. "Be careful," we calmly called out.

All of a sudden, the seals started to move. Scooting along the sand, they poured into the water. The babies and a few adults stayed on the shore.

About a dozen seals swam about twenty feet out, right in front of where Cedar and Isaac stood at the edge of the shore. The seals just stared at our kids.

Erinn and I looked at each other, wordlessly communicating our parenting questions and worries. Knowing the ways our own socialized city instincts could be impacting our fears. Were these creatures being protective? Were they angry? Were our kids safe?

I casually called out, "All right, you guys, let's start making our way back."

The kids started walking back the way we had come. To our utter surprise, the seals in the water started following us. We kept walking and they kept our pace. Always twenty feet out, staring right at us.

My nerves grew, but so did the kids' excitement. They began to run down the shore. As soon as the kids started running, we watched the seals dive under the water and pop up again farther down the beach, right where the kids had stopped. They would laugh and call out to the seals to follow them.

It happened over and over again until it was so clear that these seals were playing with the kids. They wanted to be near us. They kept us company when we took breaks and swam ahead when the kids would run. We traveled this way for over a mile along the beach.

It was magic. To play with these majestic creatures. To feel the relationship. The ways we were all paying attention to one another's moves. To communicate without language and across boundaries of water and land.

We laughed in amazement and let the joy run all the way through the veins in our body. We danced along the shore.

We could have stayed there all day, but fog was rolling in. It seemed like the weather was starting to turn. I could feel the pressure change and was starting to get a headache. Not wanting to leave, we all said our goodbyes to the seals, offering gratitude for this mystical experience. And then we turned into the beach grass and down the path where the seals could not follow.

By the time we returned to the little cabin where we were staying, it looked like the sun had set, yet it was still the middle of the afternoon. It was dark and the fog was thick. I looked up into the sky and could make out the sun in a clear vibrant orange. I shouldn't be able to look at the sun like this, I thought.

I turned on my phone and checked the weather. This was not fog. This was smoke. For the first time in my life, I was experiencing wildfire smoke. I had always thought of this as a West Coast problem. Not one of the climate catastrophes we in the Midwest (or at this moment, on the East Coast) would ever have to experience.

This would turn out to be one of many days we would experience wildfire smoke from Canada that summer. Thirty-four million acres burned. We would learn about the terror and frustration of what it meant when it was not safe to let our kids play outside, day after day.

STANDING IN THE TENSION

All in one afternoon, we experienced both overwhelming joy as we played with the seals on the edge of the ocean and overwhelming fear as the next climate crisis blew its smoke overhead.

This is the work that stands before us . . . the tension we now live in each day. We do not look away from the crisis right before us, but somehow we still find joy. We choose joy. We claim joy. Not the kind of numb happiness that comes from ignoring the pain, but the gut-wrenching, belly-aching joy that emerges from having looked it in the eye.

Mario Benedetti's glorious poem "Por Que Cantamos" names what I yearn for in my bones yet struggle to find the words for. Here is but a piece of it.

> If each hour brings death
> If time is a den of thieves
> The breezes carry a scent of evil
> And life is just a moving target
> you will ask why we sing. . .
> We sing because the river is humming
> And when the river hums
> The river hums
> We sing because cruelty has no name

But we can name its destiny
We sing because the child because everything
Because the future because the people
We sing because the survivors
And our dead want us to sing.[1]

This is the age for singing. This is the time to choose joy in the face of death. To laugh though you have considered all the facts. Joy becomes a matter of survival or, in other words, it is perhaps what keeps us alive. It is our crying out to be human in a world that is making it hard to live humanly.

Joy happens slowly and sometimes without me even noticing. The cranky old man on the corner teaches us how to grow tomatoes. Pizza devoured after an afternoon cleaning up condoms and bullets from the alley with neighbors. Handpicked cherries passed over the fence in exchange for steaming hot tamales. This post-industrial city gives way to chickens, bees, and vegetable farms. The constant companions of these children reminding me to laugh daily. I give thanks for the everyday ordinary moments, for a long history of communities practicing joy as resistance, and for knowing that joy is one thing that cannot be taken from us even as the ice caps melt and the temperatures rise.

AWE AND WONDER

"It's a portal!"

The dark had given way to light as all eight of us stepped out of the tunnel into a forest full of trees.

An hour earlier, we had been sitting around the living room. Isaac was getting bored and starting to take it out on his younger brother. And Cedar had started hanging on me asking for screen time. We had friends in town, along with their two kids. We needed a shift.

"You know, there is something I noticed out in the woods that I think we need to explore," I said taking a chance.

Five minutes later, we had shoes on and a backpack full of snacks and were headed out the door. We walked down the hill and then I turned off-trail into the woods. The kids followed in excitement. "Where are we going?" they kept asking.

"I think there is a tunnel up ahead."

"I see it!" All four kids began to run.

When the grown-ups caught up, we all stood before a ten-foot-tall culvert. It must go under the road and be used for water run-off. But it was dry in that moment. It was a long culvert. When we peered in, we mostly saw darkness with a little hole of light way at the other end.

The kids' eyes were wide open with excitement. "Let's go." And they disappeared into the dark. The grown-ups were slower to enter and slower on our feet as we felt our way through the darkness.

When we all walked out on the other end, it was as if we had entered another world. It was magic. We may have just crossed from one side of the road to the other, but for the kids, we had gone from one world to the next.

And in truth, I felt like my heart had gone from one world to the next. Witnessing their questions, their wonderment, their courage, and their joy had shifted my spirit. The way these kids see the world, the way they walk on the land, what their eyes stumble upon and their hearts notice—all of it—can pull me from exhaustion and despair toward joy and hope.

Awe and wonder are gifts my kids give me daily.

But also, I believe it is a gift we adults need to give the children in our lives.

These kids are growing up in an incredibly anxious time. Yes, the climate is changing. Weather is more extreme. The future is unpredictable. But also, there is one school shooting after another. Our kids do drills and hide in closets. And Covid . . . Covid changed everything for them . . . in an instant. Everything about these children's lives was turned upside down.

It's too much. Sure, they are resilient. But, still, it's too much. I can start to feel anger running through my veins at all these kids are holding. It's too much.

How could these kids not grow up anxious and worried and stressed and angry?

You know what is an antidote to anxiety and despair? Awe and wonder.

We *owe* our children awe and wonder!!

It is our job. It is our responsibility to find beauty in unexpected places, to marvel at the miracles around us, and to rest in moments of pure magic.

So, friends, let us—with everything we've got—make space for awe and wonder.

We need it. Awe and wonder hold our hearts and bodies in the present moment around us, keeping us from spiraling into whatever is yet to come. We can find it anywhere . . . in the streets, the woods, our neighborhoods, the shore of the ocean, or in a culvert under the road. It happens in the slowing down. It happens when we let ourselves loose. When we let go of control and are free to stumble upon joy.

Let us show these children in our lives that, amid all the horror, there is a life worth living that can take your breath away and leave you dancing.

Beloved friends,
go out and find a secret portal.
Walk the shoreline
and keep your eye out for magic.
Pull out that old telescope.
Tell wild stories.
Go outside and dance in the rain.
Do ridiculous things.
Be "that" adult who gets the eyeroll
and the side smile.
Laugh often. Slow down.
Feed the imagination.
Clear the space to be washed over
by this wild and wonderful world.

A BLESSING FOR JOY

May you listen for joy.
She is calling your name.
Lie down and put your ear to the dirt.
Feel her in the wind and the rising sun.
She is in the final breath
and the first.
She lives in the womb,
and the fire, and the pouring rain.
She is longing for you to see her standing there
and invite her in to laugh a while.

14 | RECONCEIVING OURSELVES AS CREATURES

It was the briefest of moments. If I had sneezed, I might have missed it. I heard the bathroom door and Isaac shuffled through the kitchen back to the floor where he was working on building legs for his Lego duck farm creation.

As he walked past, he called out, "Mommy, in case you are there when I die, I want my body dragged into the woods and left there. That way my body can become food for so many creatures." And just like that, he was back off to his playing.

Sometimes I am left without words or a mumbling puddle of awe when I listen to this kid.

FORGOTTEN TO WHOM WE BELONG

As this crisis intensifies in ways I could not have imagined, it feels clearer to me that at the heart of it all is the simple fact that we as humans no longer understand ourselves to be creatures that belong to this ecosystem.

We see ourselves as separate, superior. The land and animals are here to serve our survival. At best, we humans understand ourselves as caretakers of the land. Yet in reality, we are part of this land. Our fingers and toes are as beloved and necessary to this place as each leg on the cherry millipede or the wing of the monarch butterfly. We are mortal animals who impact our watershed with every breath we take. And eventually, we all become dirt.

As I write the word "humans," I know that it is not all humans. There are so many indigenous communities and people around the world who live in right relationship with the earth. It is primarily in the cultures I have known—Western, white, Christian, educated, United States citizens who operate within the belly of the beast of empire.

Over my multiple decades on this planet, this superiority has leaked its way into my consciousness as I've soaked in messages from advertisers, classrooms, politicians, and churches. I believe it is the yellow finch and the black bear that can remind us of who we really are because they have no agenda other than to coexist.

To relearn, reimagine, reconceive of myself as a two-legged being on this land, I knew who I needed to talk to. There are two creatures who live in my house who seem to have yet to forget. They understand themselves as part of a wide beloved creaturely community.

A RIPPLE IN A POND

So I asked for a conversation with Isaac and Cedar. We went out onto our porch and sat down in the shade. It was a hot muggy day, but a breeze was beginning to move through the trees. On the table beside us was a pot overflowing with basil and Cedar's beloved Venus flytrap, which he faithfully fed ticks and flies and ants he caught in the house.

I began by asking, "When you think of yourself? Do you think of yourself as a creature?"

Cedar: "Kind of."

Isaac: "Yes."

Lydia: "How would you describe that? What does it feel like?"

Isaac: "I think of myself as a creature like I am one in a million. Humans and animals are the same. Like how ants make their homes underground and we make ours above ground. We are just the same as them, just a different size with different homes."

Cedar: "Yeah everyone is related."

As they answered, a wasp began buzzing around us. It landed in Cedar's hair and then took flight again and started swirling around Isaac's head.

Isaac: "Like this wasp flying around us, out of trillions, this wasp is flying around us. It is one of us too. Animals are beings and so are people. Living beings. And trees and plants."

Cedar: "Most things have a life source inside of them."

This was a word I hadn't heard my youngest use before.

Lydia: "What is a life source?"

Cedar: "It lets you be alive. It is like yourself . . . your body."

Isaac: "People have a life source because they are alive. Plants have a life source that allows them to gather light and grow."

Cedar: "Well it's like what I read in this book . . . like if you drop a pebble, a tiny little pebble, into a pond, it will make tons of ripples. That little pond will never be the same again. So like you could think about that for yourself."

I think this kid is talking about hope. "Say more." I nudge him on.

Isaac: "One small difference and the world will never be the same."

Lydia: "Like with you in it, the world will never be the same."

Isaac: "Yes, you can make a big difference"

Cedar: "You can make the world a better place."

The wasp had continued to buzz around and landed on the table between us. We all stared at it quietly as it wet its legs in a little puddle of water.

Lydia: "Cedar, I think about how you talk about bee stings. Can you explain that?"

Cedar: "If you get stung by a honeybee, it hurts you. You could start crying. It could really hurt. But it is more sad for the bee cause it has to die. It has its heart inside its abdomen so when its stinger goes into you it gets pulled out with some of the guts which kills the bee. It is more sad for the bee than you."

Isaac: "The bee just wants to defend its group. It is born with a defense it can only use once. It's sad."

Cedar: "Like in this book I read *The Way of the Hive*, there was a woodpecker drilling into the hive and one of the bees had to go out and sting it in the eye. The woodpecker died and so did the bee. Even though the bee is so much smaller some people would say "it's so much smaller compared to the woodpecker. It won't make that much of a difference." But really it will. Like the pebble thing."

Isaac: "Small things can cause big changes. Like a single mosquito will come and bite you and then you, or at least I, will have a huge rash from the bite and then it will start bleeding and turn into a scab."

Cedar: "But while that is happening, the mosquito will go back and lay eggs."

Isaac: "It can't produce enough blood itself, so it has to use other people's."

Cedar: "Which will make the baby mosquitos, which will make more mosquitos. So sometimes you just have to let it get your blood. Cause if it doesn't get blood in time . . . imagine if they never bit you . . . because if they never got more blood, they could go extinct. So just that tiny amount of blood it gets from you keeps all the mosquitos from going extinct."

Isaac: "I kind of want mosquitos extinct."

Lydia: "Yeah, but I wonder what the consequences would be. If they did disappear, who eats the mosquitos?"

Isaac: "Frogs, spiders."

Cedar: "And then that would make everything else disappear, and then eventually the entire ecosystem would be destroyed just because of a single bit of blood in your body."

Lydia: "Yeah, if you think of the food chain, if everything began to disappear, maybe humans would disappear."

Isaac: "One small thing can make a huge difference."

Lydia: "Which makes me think, if a mosquito bite can make that big of a difference, what small differences could we make that could affect so much?"

Isaac: "We already have. Pollution. Cars."

Cedar: "Cutting down trees. Imagine if you were just a bird inside of the nest of a tree and someone cut it down. And you fell out. And imagine you had eggs and they cracked. Your kids died. You fell. You clip your wings. And then imagine all the other branches fell on you and you died."

Lydia: "What are good things that we could do that would create that kind of ripple in the pond like you were talking about? What small things could make a big change?"

Cedar: "What you could do is climb the tree and make sure nothing is inside of it and then you chop it down."

Isaac: "And you make sure you use the whole thing."

Cedar: "And be grateful."

Isaac: "Cedar, stop itching your poison ivy."

As we were talking, Cedar had started itching under his arm and down his leg and even the tip of his nose. The oil was surely spreading. Cedar gave Isaac a dirty look. I brought the conversation back, "What are other things?"

Cedar: "Planting other greens. You could put birdseed every-where for birds, chipmunks, and squirrels in the winter so they don't have to work as hard to find food."

Lydia: "I think a lot of our problems in the world are because most people don't think of themselves as part of the earth. They go out and enjoy nature, but they aren't part of nature. Like I am a human being and those are animals, but I am not an animal. You know what I mean? Why do you think humans think they are so much better?"

Isaac: "Because humans are not as smart. Humans are part of nature."

Cedar: "Everything in the world is part of nature."

Isaac: "Things that humans do might not be part of nature like pollution. Pollution kills nature and destroys."

Cedar: "Yeah that's the opposite of nature."

Isaac: "Humans can have two sides. One that is part of nature and one against it."

Lydia: "I wonder like with pollution, if human beings saw themselves as nature, maybe they wouldn't make pollution. Because they would see themselves as part of the earth. What would the world look like if we thought of ourselves as creatures? What would be different?"

Cedar: "It would be a lot greener."

Isaac: "Fewer trees would be cut down."

Cedar: "Yeah, there would be a lot more wildlife."

Isaac: "People would probably live in smaller houses. Not really using money. If you want to get something, get it yourself. Like if you need wood, cut down a tree. Then if humans knew they were animals, they would be friends with other animals. And animals wouldn't be as afraid of humans."

Cedar: "Yeah, animals wouldn't be afraid of you."

Isaac: "We would bond. You could go ride a deer."

Cedar: "Or have dinner with a bear."

Lydia: "How do you think we get back to that? How do we get humans to think of ourselves as creatures?"

Cedar: "You could rename yourself a name of a kind of a tree . . . like me. Then you could think of yourself as a tree and then you don't want to go cut down a tree because you are a tree too. If you chop down a tree, it is like imagining if someone came and cut you down."

Lydia: "Wow. So do you think that because your name is Cedar, you feel closer to trees?"

Cedar: "Maybe. Ah! There is a daddy longlegs on your chair. 'Hey big daddy.'"

We pause to admire the insect crawling up Isaac's chair. Yesterday, we noticed the Venus flytrap had caught a daddy longlegs and all we could see left were a few legs sticking out from the hairy fibers of the plant.

Lydia: "Isaac, one thing you talk about that shows how you think of yourself as a creature is when you talk about how, when you die, you want to put your body in the woods and become food for other animals."

Isaac: "Yeah, use it up."

Lydia: "Not many people think like that. A lot of people want to be put in a metal box and put underground separate from the dirt and the bugs. The idea that when we die we actually become a gift to our ecosystem . . . that means we are a creature."

Isaac: "I want to become of some use when I die. I don't just want to be wasted."

Cedar: "Yeah don't just waste your body. You can have a good life and a good death."

Shivers flow through my body. "Well," I say. "I think you are a good animal."

Isaac: "I think you make a good chicken."

Cedar: "I think your face makes a good pig."
Isaac: "I think you make a good blob fish."

And just like that, the moment passed. But here among the basil and the daddy longlegs, the wasps and the poison ivy, and my two sweet children, I was relearning to feel the weight of my body in this place. As Mary Oliver says, I was learning to let the "soft animal of my body love what it loves."[1]

And as this book begins to wind its way toward the end, it feels right to let these two young ones' voices weave across the page with all their wisdom, noticings, and humor. We need it all. We need all the children born into this moment in time to be part of the voice and imagination that leads us forward. Without pressure or expectation, we welcome them just as they are. And we offer them just who we are—animals, with all our foibles and misconceptions.

Dear friends,
Go to the places where you most feel like an animal.
Lie down beside the ant hill,
climb an old apple tree,
or soak your feet in the shallowness of the lake
'til the minnows come to nibble on your toes.
Release your superiority.
Reject empire's claims.
Go have dinner with a bear
. . . or maybe not.
But remember the mosquito babies
and the birds in the fallen trees.
Be like the pig and the blob fish.
Rejoice in your wild, mortal flesh.

A BLESSING FOR YOUR CREATURELY BODY

Oh, beautiful creature,
breathe into your body,
deep into the caverns of your life force.
And as you exhale,
remember that you are
feeding the trees.
With each breath
your creatureliness
meets another.
Become part of the forest.
Just like a ripple in the pond,
your existence here,
along with the honeybee and the cedar tree,
leaves this world forever changed.

CONCLUSION
After the Rain Fell

The power didn't come back on for days. And the water on the freeway did not subside.

Each morning, we would wake up and walk down the street to see if the water was still there.

Without air-conditioning or the glowing screens of entertainment, we all stayed outside looking for a bit of relief from the heat, under the maple trees and with good company. We would gather at the end at the freeway with lawn chairs and picnic baskets.

Our entertainment soon consisted of watching three tow trucks attempt to pull the semi-truck out of the water over the course of three days. It was a clumsy experiment that went late into the night. There was lots of cheering and groaning and laughing.

It didn't take much squinting to feel like we lived beside a large river. At sunset, the water rippled and the tall (uncut) grasses along the embankment danced in the wind. It was beautiful. We all realized we would much prefer to live beside a river rather than along this noisy, smelly highway. Across the way, a couple of kids brought a canoe down the exit ramp and began to paddle until the police pulled it out.

On the second day, when it was clear the power wasn't coming back, we all opened our freezers and pulled grills out onto our front lawns. It was a feast. Steak, hot dogs, hamburgers, veggie dogs, and all the ice cream you could eat.

One neighbor pulled out a tuba and was quickly joined by another neighbor with a clarinet who hadn't played since high school.

We checked in on elders and those with health concerns. Kids biked in the street. Some napped in lawn chairs.

It was a festival.

No one was naïve to the gravity of the situation or confused about the larger implications for our planet . . . including my kids. Yet here we were, able to find joy and community in the midst of it all.

I don't think it would be an exaggeration to say that the neighborhood saved me. I think I would have long ago fallen into a puddle of misery and anxiety.

WHAT'S NEXT?

After six days, the water disappeared. Two more days and the tow trucks had carried away the cars that were exposed beneath. A few weeks and even the trash and water lines disappeared.

And quickly, everything seemed to go back to normal. We kept filling our gas tanks and entering that freeway. We kept buying crappy food from the corporate chains. We left lights on and used more water than we needed.

It was easy to forget.

Just one more small, localized climate catastrophe. They are happening every day. Here and there. You've probably felt them yourself. Too smoky to go outside. Too dangerous to drink the water. Too cold to leave the house. Not enough water to water your garden. Evacuation orders.

It is touching us all. And yet, I fear that "normal" is too seductive. Our memory too forgetful. Will we wake up?

Where are we headed?

One possibility is that we get this right. We let our imaginations carry us and our love of this world drive us. And we shift . . . we transition death-dealing profit systems to life-giving generous systems. We learn to live in new ways and it's marvelous.

Another possibility is that we don't get it right. Weather gets more volatile. Politics get more deadly. Systems crumble. And we face into the worst.

I don't know. I can oscillate between both and a million possibilities in the middle.

What I do know is that either way doesn't change how I want to live. I want to fight like hell and grow tomatoes. I want to worship with the praying mantis and learn how to build composting toilets. I want to play with my kids and sing in the wind. I want to honor the dead and feed the birds.

Either way doesn't change that there can be joy and laughter, awe and wonder, love and community. Either way sharpens my gaze on what matters and what just doesn't. Either way I want to live humanly and invite our kids into deeper knowing of what it means to be alive on this sweet earth. That is not a bad life and one for which I, as a parent, can give thanks.

FINAL FOOD FOR THOUGHT

"Mommy, I want my body dragged into the woods and left there so my body can become food for creatures."

The phrase repeats in my mind over and over, like a sacred mantra.

One day my body will feed the trees. I will nourish this sacred ecosystem that I love so much. I have been loved and nourished and kept alive by this place. And one day my breath will stop. And I will become food for the creatures tucked in the soil. I will strengthen the topsoil and my minerals will rise up through the trees into the flowers and fruit.

My death will be a gift to the earth. I will become new life for a future not my own.

I don't know where we are going or what will happen. I don't know how long humanity will survive.

But let us be a gift for whatever time we have left. Let us sing to the trees. And dance under the stars. Let us tend to gardens. And walk gently in the grasses. Let us cry out for liberation. Let us laugh and cry and listen to these sweet and fierce children.

And if all else fails, or when all this is done, may we meet sister death with welcome. In our own death or in the death of humanity, our bodies will tend the earth. We will be good food . . . for whatever is to come.

EPILOGUE
To Look Out My Window

As I tinker with the last words of this book, there is a vivid yellow finch that keeps landing in the pine tree out my office window. It has come every day for the last week. It sits on the branch for a while and then flies and lands right on the tip of the narrow windowsill. It sits there and looks at me. And then flies away. Each time he leaves, I say a prayer that he will come again and I give thanks for this visit. I know he keeps returning for a reason, I just don't know what yet. But I know I need him.

Beyond the pine tree I look out to see mountains. Rolling hills and a ridge in the distance. I watch from above as the turkey vultures circle the trees below. I can see the shadows cast among the trees made by the clouds above. We are no longer in Detroit.

This is my home now. It is very different from the view of our scrappy urban backyard filled with projects made from makeshift supplies we would find on the curb.

A year ago, we made the terrifying decision to pack up our beloved life in Detroit and move to Kirkridge Retreat and Study Center in Bangor, Pennsylvania, along the Kittatinny Ridge.

Kirkridge is a place I had loved for a long time. My sister and I grew up regularly running around on the mountain or lying on the huge stones or marveling at the ice-covered trees. It has long been a place for peace activism and theological imagination. My parents attended the retreats and we snuck hot chocolate and loved the land. My parents fell in love on a car ride to Kirkridge when my dad was hitchhiking to a retreat and my mom decided to give him a ride. Kirkridge is the backdrop to one of only pieces of video footage we have of my mom. It is a tape I have watched over and over these past eighteen years since she died.

When I was a kid, I would often find myself on the outskirts of organizing meetings with Grace Boggs. I can still hear her voice ask as she so often did, "What time is it on the clock of the world?"

That is the question that lingers deep in my gut. The choice for us to move from our Detroit neighborhood to total Pennsylvania was about listening to that question and imagining how we could respond.

As I stepped into the work at this retreat center with a long history of centering the voices of LGBTQ folks, doing the work of peacemaking, and tending to this beautiful land, I wanted to be awake to how this place could be needed and offered in this moment and in the days to come.

Moving away from the city I had lived in most of my life was one of the hardest things I have ever done, but this move also felt right for so many reasons. Many of those reasons are the longings and commitments I write about in this book. We wanted to live closer to earth. Feel our bodies shift with the rhythms of the season. Create space for hospitality. Dream into visions for climate resilience. Grow food. Put up solar. Learn how to build strawbale. Build composting toilets.

Our kids have made some clear asks of us over the years. There are moments when their conscience seems to be speaking so strongly to them that we need to listen. There was a time when Isaac begged us to bike instead of drive because of the pollution. Not easy to do in the car capital of the world, but we worked hard to listen to his cry. In part, this move feels like listening to our kids' desires to be closer to the earth and find ways to live with more reciprocity.

We brought both kids into the discernment process. I brought them with me to my interview and said, "If you don't love this place, we will take that very seriously." But they did. And when the job offer came, the four of us sat down and went around the circle each saying yes. Then we made the acceptance call together.

While the transition has not all been easy and there has been a lot of grief, the kids have totally and completely fallen in love with this place and our rhythms of work and hospitality.

The first time someone asked Isaac what he loved about living here, he replied, "That there is less pollution when you go outside." My heart sank. He had been carrying the weight of air quality with him each day and he was feeling a little lighter as he breathed in the mountain air. My heart also sank with something more akin to anger knowing the privilege of moving out of the city. Environmental racism has its grasp around Detroit. The struggle for climate justice can never ever be separated from racial justice or economic justice. It is one fight.

It felt complicated to finish this book that was set so lovingly in our years in Detroit from another watershed. I felt the tension of encouraging readers to put down roots and think about place-based living while I was in the midst of a move myself. It is not a move we took lightly. Moving our bodies out of Detroit was full of so much grief. And we are still learning the land we now stand on.

It took a while to learn that we were not pulling up our roots as much as leaving our roots there and becoming seeds. Our roots will always be in that city even as we put down new roots in this place.

This book in so many ways is a love letter to Detroit and to Larkins Street. It is the place where I learned about community and resistance, about justice and joy, and about life and death. It is the place I was born and the place where I wept over my mother's dead body. It is the place where both Isaac and Cedar were born. Those streets formed my politics and my theological imagination.

I miss that old view out my window. The plum tree I was pruning when my contractions began with Isaac. The tree fort the kids built with their grandpa. The swing set given a second life, brought to our yard piece by piece. The chickens on the hunt for green leaves and tasty bugs. The fire pit Erinn and I built with bricks we had found in the alley, which was used for Samhains and potlucks. And that beautiful homemade pizza oven that made the sweetest pizza you ever tasted. I love that place. I poured my heart and sweat, my laughter and my tears into that tiny stretch of land. I am forever changed by loving that place. I will always feel my belonging to that land no matter where I go. The work going forward will be on the Kittatinny Ridge, named by the Lenape as "endless mountain," whose formations stretch back four hundred and fifty million years. But it will also always be in hopes of justice, beauty, and resilience for that stretch of dirt in southwest Detroit.

A BLESSING FROM
THE SEASONS

Spring
when buckets of sap hang from the maple trees
and the tiny snow bells beckon our delight
and that sweet taste of asparagus and strawberries
and that first warm breeze on your face
and the fruit trees that burst with blossoms
and the lilacs wafting in through the window
make it almost impossible
to feel anything other than
hope.

Summer
when the world turns vibrant green
and juice pours from the first slice of a tomato
and your body resting in relief on the rise of the waves
and summer thunder reverberates through your body
and baskets overflow with peppers and basil and cucumbers
and zucchini so big you don't know what to do with it
makes it almost impossible
not to feel like the world is full of
abundance.

Autumn
when the colors shift on the tips of the leaves
and you can smell life return to dirt
and leaves crunch beneath your feet
and pantries fill with jars of tomato sauce and raspberry
    jam
and the bears fill their bellies
and the smell of apples and cinnamon rising from our
    kitchens
makes it almost impossible
not to feel
held.

Winter
when we are gifted that blanket of darkness
and frost kisses our cheeks
and everything grows still
and branches painted against the sky expose the hunting
    hawks
and the seeds are at rest in the blackness below our feet
and snow covers the ground and branches of the trees
makes it almost impossible
not to feel
home.

And yet as icicles grow along the edges of rocks and roofs
spring will come again
and summer after that
and autumn once more.
And while I trust in the certainty of change
from one season to the next,

nothing is predictable anymore.
Not even the changing seasons themselves.
Take nothing for granted.
Stand in awe.
Clothe yourselves
in the beauty of this world.

ACKNOWLEDGMENTS

I ache with gratitude for all the creatures and plants that have been my companions on the little corner in Southwest Detroit. For the opossums, the black squirrels, the raccoons. The chickens, the blue jays, the red-tailed hawks, the yellow finches, the cardinals, the chickadees, the downy woodpeckers, and the pigeons. For the wild ginger, the bleeding heart, the milkweed, the woodruff, the raspberries, the rhubarb, the tiger lilies, and the phlox. For the peach trees, the cherry trees, the apple trees, the apricot trees, and the grape vines. I have grown to know you in the changing of the seasons. Thank you for teaching me about who I am. Thank you for letting me love you. Thank you for your beauty, your food, your relationships. I hope that our feet upon that land and the work of our hands were gifts in return.

I am so grateful for all those who read these words along the way and offered feedback—Rose Berger, Laurel Dykstra, Kate Foran, Lucia Wylie-Eggert, Bill Wylie-Kellermann, Joyce Hollyday, Erinn Fahey, and Michael McGregor at Collegeville Institute. I trust your wise creaturely beings so much. Thank you to everyone at Broadleaf Books who just make the work of writing such terrific fun.

I also want to add gratitude for those whom Erinn and I walk alongside in the work of parenting amid climate collapse.

There are so many, but I want to name a few. Thank you to Kate Foran and Steve Borla, Em Jacoby and Brian Klassen, Michelle Martinez, Marcia Lee and en sawyer, and especially to my sister Lucy and brother-in-law Daniel Wylie-Eggert. And thanks to all those grown-ups who love on our kids and hold these questions with us—Tom Molina, Bryan Victor, Erika Fox, Joan Smith, Joyce Hollyday, Bill Ramsey, Nichola Torbett, Ben Beautel-Gunn, Hannah Glatz, Denise Griebler, and Luke Mattson, to name a few. And for all those who have and will lay their hands on our kids' lives: By the time this book is in your hands, I know this list will have changed and feel incomplete. Gratitude for wide and growing communities.

Erinn, I love you with my whole heart. You are on every page and I am so grateful that whatever lies before us is something we get to embrace together. There is no one else I'd rather walk beside into a cataclysmic crisis.

And Isaac and Cedar, I have no words big enough for how grateful I am for both of you. Your beings have changed the fabric of my being. I love who you were, who you are, and who you will become. I love that we get to do this thing called life together. May you always feel known and loved by your Mama and me, and by the wind and the stones and the chickadees.

These stories were printed with permission and delight by Isaac and Cedar who are now ten and seven. Writing about children is a complicated thing which raises ethical questions around privacy, permission, and power. I hope that these stories will always feel to them like I honored their beings and that they feel my love wrapped around their shoulders.

It was my amazing editor, Lisa Klaskin, who came up with the title for *This Sweet Earth*. She picked it out of a sentence tucked deep in the back. It felt right. I sent it to my dad for his feedback and he responded with an email full of poetry. Some his and some Daniel Berrigan's, a Jesuit peace activist who has joined the ancestors. He wrote, "I think you got that phrase from me. And I think I got it from Dan."

I am sure he is right, but I would not have been able to name that. I love that about words and stories. Words run through me from one generation to the next. Sometimes, when I am writing and I choose a particular word, I can hear people I love coming onto the page. Some of those are beloved in the flesh and others are those I've only ever known through their words. I think to myself, *Oh, that is Joanna Macy, Laurel Dykstra, Marcia Lee, Samuel Wylie, Liz McAlister, Grace Boggs, Wendell Berry, Michelle Martinez, Martin Luther King Jr., Dorothy Day, Peter Maurin, Rose Berger, Ched Myers, Robin Wall Kimmer, Dee Dee Risher, or Mary Oliver.* On and on.

But most of the time, it is my mom's or my dad's words I hear. I love that their words have taken root within me, bringing with them stories and commitments and longings. I am so grateful. And the fact that the title comes through generations of beloved poets is all the sweeter.

I give thanks for all those whose words have formed me consciously or unconsciously, named or unnamed. None of the words you hold in your hands are mine. It has all been passed down. And will just keep going on long after these pages have returned to the earth.

FURTHER READING

If I could gift you a basket full of books

As these final pages near the end, I am mindful of little tidbits that I would love to leave with you. A few of those are books. Books that I love as a grown-up and that I love reading to my children. The gifts of stories and art have such an enormous power in shifting and shaping who we become. May we never underestimate the power of beauty.

I would so love to sit around a table together, swapping our favorite earthy books and reading them aloud to one another. I imagine we could create a long, wonderful list. But for now, here are just a few that I really, really love and want to make sure you know about.

The Harmony Tree: A Story of Healing and Community
By Randy Woodley. Illustrated by Ramone Romero.
(Friesens Press, 2016)

This is one of those books I buy in bulk and gift to all the beloved new babies in my life. It makes me cry each time I sift through the pages. It is the story of an old grandmother oak who is the only remaining tree after the forest is cut down. Yet it seeps with the power of community, the power of story, and the possibility of transformation. Under it all lies the truth of colonization and the broken relationship of settlers with indigenous communities and the land. Yet, acorns fall, carrying hope that we may be moving into a new time of healing.

Everybody Needs a Rock
By Byrd Baylor.
Illustrated by Peter Parnall
(Aladdin, 1985)

I love rocks. Holding them and searching for them, I am mindful of the stories and memory they hold. This book lays out how to find the perfect rock just for you. I find myself pulling it off the shelf and reading it to kids and adults . . . and then sending them off into the woods to wander and return with a beloved rock.

We Are Water Protectors
By Carole Lindstrom. Illustrated
by Michaela Goade.
(Roaring Book Press, 2020)

This gorgeously illustrated book honors the indigenous-led movements across North America that are leading the cry to protect our waters—from pipelines to pollution to privatization. In Detroit, surrounded by 20 percent of the world's fresh water, we experienced again and again the attack on water. Moves by corporations to soak up bottled water or plans to privatize the whole water system. We experienced the lead poisoning in Flint and the water shutoffs in Detroit. Water is the frontline of this struggle and indigenous communities are teaching all of us the way towards courage and resistance.

The Curious Garden
By Peter Brown

This book is beautiful in its simplicity. As a child finds an old train track and plants and tends a few seeds, the garden begins to spread around the whole town. As I look at the pictures, I feel the echoes of postindustrial Detroit. Both in the gloom of empty factories and poisoned land . . . but also in the ways the urban agricultural movement spread through the city, building community in its wake. And like all my favorite children's books, it points to the power of children nudging them toward those places of joy and imagination. Belief that children can change everything.

The Lost Words
By Robert Macfarlane.
Illustrated by Jackie Morris
(Anansi International, 2018)

I referenced this book in early chapters. It is big and gorgeous and full of poetry. You cannot help but run your fingers across the pages, falling in love with each plant and creature. Each page offers illustrations and poetry to one of the words that has been removed from the *Oxford Junior Dictionary* because it is no longer considered relevant to children's language needs. Acorn.

Dandelion. Otter. Willow. It is a book to sit with, to weep with, to fall in love with, and to resist by learning these words by heart.

> *How to Change Everything: The Young Human's*
> *Guide to Protecting the Planet and Each Other*
> By Rebecca Stefoff and Naomi Klein
> (Atheneum Books for Young Reader, 2022)

Over the last few weeks, my ten-year-old, Isaac, has asked me to start reading this aloud to him each night. It has become one of my favorite times of the day. Naomi Klein has been such a clear and powerful voice for so long and I love hearing her speak directly to my child's grief, mind, and power. The book speaks clearly the truth about climate change without sugarcoating anything. And yet, it is also filled with stories we so rarely hear in our media about the powerful and creative actions of young people all over the world. In the very first pages, readers are given a definition of climate justice, making the work of racial, economic, and eco justice inexplicably bound together. Somewhere amid the magnitude of it all, there is palpable hope that we really could change everything.

May stories flow like rivers summoning us into our life's work on this sweet earth.

DREAMS TAKING ROOT AT KIRKRIDGE

Just a few words to say a little more about the place and dreams that I am stepping into here at Kirkridge Retreat and Study Center.[1] Feel it as an invitation. Come rest and heal and dream on this mountain! There is work to be done.

Kirkridge Retreat and Study Center is a refuge for everyone seeking to live humanly in a violent world. It is a place of rest and recovery, an incubator of collective freedom projects, and a wilderness school where we learn to assume our right-sized place in the wild and diverse ecosystems we inhabit, recognizing that some of us have been socialized to play too big and some too small. We are serious about dismantling supremacy of every kind, at every level, and about welcoming people of all races, ethnicities, genders, sexual orientations, ages, religions, and abilities.

LAND ACKNOWLEDGMENT

Kirkridge is a sacred place. I often think about the stones that cover the ground . . . about the stories they have heard, the songs they have listened to, the tears they have held. This land holds long memories and it welcomes us here now. The stones have held the history of Kirkridge for over eighty years now, but they also hold much older stories, including those of the Lenape.

We began this book with a land acknowledgment of the Anishinaabe in Wawiatanong, and so we end with a land acknowledgment of the Lenape peoples here in Pennsylvania.

We recognize the Lenape people as the indigenous people of this land and the perennial spiritual stewards of their homelands. We commit ourselves to actively making repair for the harm done to our Lenape relatives, to being in right relationship with them, to walking well and carefully on this land, and to doing whatever we can to contribute to the thriving and sovereignty of both the Lenape people and this vibrant ecosystem.

THE DREAMS THAT CALLED ME HOME

In my first month here at Kirkridge, I wrote down these dreams for Kirkridge. They are the dreams that summoned my body to this land. Slowly you can see many of them take root. Lots more work and life to come.

I dream of a resting place.
Systems are crumbling.
The powers are wreaking havoc.
The climate is in crisis.
It is enough to make you weep.
Enough to make you scream.
It is enough for bodies to fall down in exhaustion.
Fall down here. Rest here.
Let this be a place where we can breathe, heal, and hold
    one another.

Let the stones receive our silence, our tears, our laughter,
    and our singing.

I dream about the land.
Wondering what she is whispering to our spirits?
How can we learn from this ridge in a time of climate
    change?
I dream of environmental justice organizing,
retreats on eco-spirituality and the wilderness prophets,
skill training on canning, permaculture, foraging, and cob
    building.
I dream of composting toilets, solar power, and pizza ovens.

I dream of a garden overflowing with tomatoes and basil.
A garden that feeds the kitchens,
where the land gets inside of us.

I dream of a place that lights the imagination,
that takes craft seriously.
Crafting is a form of resistance,
an act of soul tending,
a form of ancestry remembrance,
and practical survival skills.
Come make pottery, carve spoons, stitch quilts, and weave
    baskets.

I dream of an intentional community.
Beloveds who live on this land
and lean into a vocation of hospitality.
Sharing rhythms of work, spirituality, and play
connected with the wider local community.

I dream of a place that is always gathering circles
to discern the signs of the time.
In Grace Lee Boggs's words, "What time is it on the clock
    of the world?"
How do we respond? How do we resist?
How do we tend to our souls?

I dream of a place where actions are imagined,
organizing happens,
and resistance is embodied.
A place where we ask what does the spirit of
"picket and pray" mean right now?

I dream of an intergenerational landscape,
where the children and elders are our teachers.
A place that takes young folks' dreams seriously.
But also where we can hold one another in old age,
love one another,
and ask what it means to die well.

I dream of a place that will continue to welcome LGBTQ
    folks
and tell the amazing history that has happened here,
that will honor queer voices at the forefront of theology.

I dream of a place that does the hard and crucial work of
    racial justice,
internally within the organization and in our wider work,
a space that can nurture racial healing.

I dream about ways to fall more in love with the little patch
    of earth

to be quiet among the trees,
to be in relationship with the toads and the snakes and the
   deer.
I want to hide swings and benches deep in the forest.
I want to build an outdoor chapel tucked away in the
   stones.

I dream of singing and stories,
bonfires and sledding,
instruments playing and bread breaking.
I dream of births and deaths
and all the ordinary that lies between.

More than anything, I mean
to stay awake
and to love this land.[2]

100 PRACTICAL IDEAS

Looking for some ideas to spark the imagination? Some projects you can do with children?

Here is the beginning of a list. It is not comprehensive. It is not a recipe. You can add to it. And of course, you are likely already doing some of these, while others may sound like madness. Do things your own way. There is no right way to enter these times. There is no checklist. All you can do is love the land where you stand, pay attention, let your heart break, and welcome the day to come.

1. Start an indoor herb garden.

2. Find a sit spot outside that you can return to again and again.

3. Build a composting toilet.

4. Research where your trash goes. Visit if you can.

5. Go solar.

6. Bike. Get a bike trailer to haul groceries.

7. Dig up your lawn and plant native plants.

8. Plant a tree when a baby is born. Measure them up against each other year after year.

9. Find out where your electricity comes from.

10. Use gray water to flush your toilet.

11. Harvest wild edibles along your walks.

12. Make your own laundry detergent.

13. Make nature art.

14. Write a love letter to your favorite body of water.

15. Hang a bird feeder.

16. Find a tree to share your secrets with.

17. Go off-trail.

18. Dance in the rain.

19. Carry a stone in your pocket.

20. Go morel hunting in the spring.

21. Carry bird/bug/tree/mushroom identification books in your bag.

22. Make a nature shelf or altar in your house that changes each season.

23. Get a few baby chicks. Build a small chicken coop.

24. Learn beekeeping.

25. Join a food co-op.

26. Pick one night a week that you don't use any electricity.

27. Recycle.

28. Read Mary Oliver.

29. Buy a farm share.

30. Go to nature classes at the park.

31. Have a bonfire.

32. Buy local.

33. Play outside with your kids.

34. Join a protest.

35. Learn some more names of your neighbors.

36. Throw a funeral for a fallen sparrow.

37. Stop shopping on Amazon.

38. Put your phone in a different room.

39. Ask to borrow a couple of eggs from a neighbor.

40. Write your representative.

41. Slow down.

42. Work less.

43. Squander time outside.

44. Join mutual aid projects.

45. Stargaze.

46. Pray for the ice caps.

47. Learn the principles of environmental justice.

48. Make plans for your own death. Green burial?

49. Memorize jokes.

50. Sing in the wind.

51. Make violet syrup.

52. Try a digital detox.

53. Host a clothing swap party.

54. Join Freecycle. Find a free store.

55. Write poetry.

56. Show up when young people call for protests.

57. Gather wildflowers for your kitchen.

58. Write a land acknowledgment.

59. Compost.

60. Use reusable bags.

61. Mend clothes.

62. Write your spiritual autobiography that traces your life by the trees you have known.

63. Play board games.

64. Read books of history about the place you live.

65. Host potlucks.

66. Go skinny-dipping.

67. Use the library.

68. Learn from indigenous organizations in your area.

69. Read the newspaper.

70. Build an outdoor pizza oven.

71. Rest in the sunshine.

72. Talk to animals.

73. Swim in a stream.

74. Follow the lead of children.

75. Repair toys and stuffed animals.

76. Lie down in the snow.

77. East less meat. Eat no meat.

78. Stop buying bottled water.

79. Take off your shoes and put your feet in the mud.

80. Repair your toaster.

81. Learn your ancestry.

82. Hang laundry.

83. Plant a memorial garden.

84. Laugh.

85. Read a book.

86. Listen to the story of an elder.

87. Make homemade gifts.

88. If it's yellow, let is mellow. If it's brown, flush it down.

89. Learn a new craft.

90. Scream off the top of a mountain.

91. Quit your job and find a way to do what you love.

92. Light that fire at the same moon each year.

93. Carry birdseed gifts out into the forest.

94. Wait to make your favorite soup 'til the first snowfall.

95. Save seeds from your vegetable garden.

96. Write ten things you are grateful for each day.

97. Write your obituary.

98. Read Ayisha Siddiqa's "On another Panel about Climate, They Ask Me to Sell the Future and All I've Got Is a Love Poem"

99. Say you are sorry to the blue whale and the snow leopard and the red panda.

100. Take a nap.

A GATHERED
WATERSHED PRAYER

Instructions: Go out on a walk with kids and gather the items below. You can physically gather some of them to bring back in a bouquet or create an altar. And some creatures you will just need to find and write the names down.

If there are creatures or plants you don't know, let this be an opportunity to look them up and learn their names.

Once you have gathered with your eyes and hands, fill in the spaces in the prayer from the list you gathered. It is OK if you don't find everything, just weave in the items or write in something you know lives in your watershed.

Flowers
    1. _____
    2. _____

Birds
    1. _____
    2. _____

Trees
    1. _____
    2. _____

Bugs

   1. _____

   2. _____

Seeds/Nuts

   1. _____

   2. _____

Creatures or Other Nature Finds

   1. _____

   2. _____

PRAYER

Oh spirit,
who dwells in the _____ and the _____.
                   (bug)   (tree)
We greet you in the call of the _____.
                                 (bird)
We give thanks for this day and the ways you live all around
   us.
Your power and imagination rests in the tiny_____.
                                   (type of seed)
You surprise us in the wind
   and nourish us with the rain.
May we always remember right down to your toes
   that this whole ecosystem with each
         _____ and _____.
       (flower)   (bird or nature find)

loves us and is glad we are part of this
wild and wonderful place.

Let us live each day in a way that honors the
_____ and _____.
     (bug)   (creature)

NOTES

INTRODUCTION

1 Bayo Akomolafe, "A Slower Urgency." https://rb.gy/kh2253
2 To learn more, see "Waawiyatanong: A Detroit Land Acknowledgment," Antonio Cosme, *Geez* Magazine, Issue 55, Winter 2020. https://rb.gy/s5xk5y

CHAPTER 2

1 Lydia Wylie-Kellermann, "Elders and Children Lay Their Hands Upon Us Now," *Geez* Magazine, Issue 54, Fall 2019. https://rb.gy/kh2253
2 https://rb.gy/kh2253
3 Marcia Lee and en sawyer, "Building Community: Choosing Life in the Certainty of Death," in *The Sandbox Revolution*, Lydia Wylie-Kellermann, ed. (Minneapolis: Broadleaf Books, 2021), 192.

CHAPTER 3

1 "In the end, we will conserve only what we love, we will love only what we understand, and we will understand only what we are taught." Baby Dioum at the General Assembly of the IUCN (International Union for Conservation of Nature) held in New Delhi in 1968.

2 "Nearly Three Billion Birds Have Gone Missing." https://www.birds.cornell.edu/home/bring-birds-back/.

CHAPTER 4

1 Jarrod McKenna and Joanna Shenk, "Vincent Harding (episode 46)," 5/6/2013, in the *Iconocast*, podcast, https://www.jesusradicals.com/iconocast/vincent-harding

CHAPTER 5

1 Arthur Waskow, *Seasons of Our Joy: A Celebration of Modern Jewish Renewal.* (Boston: Beacon Press, 1982), ix.

CHAPTER 6

1 "Dad's Goodbye to Lydia before Palestine." Cassette, 1990.

CHAPTER 8

1 Grace Lee Boggs, *The Next American Revolution: Sustainable Activism for the Twenty-First Century*, (Berkeley, CA: University of California Press, 2012), xxi.
2 Krista Tippet, "John Lewis: Love in Action," March 28, 2013, in *On Being*, podcast, https://tinyurl.com/3rmmzt6z.
3 Boggs, *American Revolution*, 134.
4 Boggs, *American Revolution*, 96.
5 Boggs, *American Revolution*, 164–5.

CHAPTER 11

1 See more at "What Would happen if all the nuclear bombs were detonated?" BBC Science Focus, https://rb.gy/kh2253 and "Nuclear Weapons Worldwide," Union of Concerned Scientists, https://tinyurl.com/sxncpxc5.

CHAPTER 13

1 Printed with permission from D'Arcy Martin and Between the Lines Publishing. "Why We Sing" by Mario Benedetti, translated by D'Arcy Martin. *Educating for Change*, Rick Arnold, ed. (Toronto: Between the Lines and the Doris Marshall Institute for Education and Action, 1991), 6.

CHAPTER 14

1 Mary Oliver, "Wild Geese," in *Dream Work*, (New York: Atlantic Monthly Press, 1986).

DREAMS TAKING ROOT AT KIRKRIDGE

1 Learn more about Kirkridge Retreat and Study Center at www.kirkridge.org or email lydiawk@kirkridge.org.
2 Lydia Wylie-Kellermann, "The Dreams That Called Me Home," written for a Kirkridge fall festival and shared through email and letter to the wider community.